A Modern-Day Guide to Homeschooling for Everyone

HOME SCHOOL *happily*

YES, YOU CAN!

LAURA KRONEN

BeYouOnlyBetter.com | ATLANTA, GA

Printed in the United States of America

First Printing, 2020

ISBN 978-1-7351473-2-1 Paperback
ISBN 978-1-7351473-3-8 ebook

Published by Be You Only Better®, LLC
Cover Design and Interior Formatting by Becky's Graphic Design®, LLC

DEDICATION

To my little loves,
who have grown into the
most extraordinary young men.

I am beyond grateful to have been able to spend
this time together teaching you, inspiring you,
and watching you learn.

I love you the most!

Table of Contents

foreword

Everyone thought I was going mad when I said that I was going to homeschool my children four years ago. Yet the level of respect for us homeschool moms went up about 100 percent when our country shut down, and we were all quarantined in place because of the wicked coronavirus that swept across our extraordinary planet. Those same people that had criticized and questioned me in 2016 were now asking for help with curricula and for advice to keep their children on track because public schools were not providing work promptly or giving them challenging enough lessons. Others needed guidance because a significant percentage of our nation's students were left high and dry in the middle of Advanced Placement (AP) classes, and their children needed to prepare for upcoming AP exams, which would count toward college credit. Many other parents contacted me, asking me how I had the patience to do this because they were going to lose their collective minds. Was there a magic elixir they could drink?

All of these parents thought they were now *homeschooling* their children because their son or daughter was sitting at the kitchen table doing work. All of the social media posts with #thisishomeschooling, #homeschoolmom, and #homeschooling started to grate on my nerves. (Or it could have been the fact that I couldn't leave the house and I was becoming slightly unhinged. That could do it.) At any rate, that was not homeschooling; that was homework, and there is a colossal difference. I wanted to ask all of these parents if they painstakingly created yearlong syllabuses for their child and wrote daily agendas. Or if they constructed PowerPoints on different subjects? Graded their papers? Planned multiple field trips and other events to enrich their learning? Or did they simply print out school-supplied worksheets and sit their child in front of a laptop to complete school-assigned activities?

You see, real homeschooling does not occur in isolation like when we are confined to our homes, and it is not exclusively online. It includes real-world activities and social events, and is based on a child and their parent's interests. It also occurs at your child's own pace, and it should be fun! But I bit my tongue and never asked those questions. (OK, maybe I did—but only once or twice.) I realized the world didn't need my snarky attitude when a virus was wiping out tens of thousands of people.

> "
> From the day you became a parent, you also became a teacher —you are made for this!
>
> LAURA KRONEN

What was happening at home was *quarantine schooling*, also known as *pandemic schooling* or *crisis schooling*. Does it lessen the value of a parent helping their child at home? No, definitely not. But there is a stark contrast between homeschooling as a seasoned homeschool parent knows it to be and the uncharted territory that other parents were thrown into, having not made the conscious choice to homeschool. In light of this, I think the crisis our world endured will have a categorically positive effect on growing our homeschool community. Almost every parent across the globe was introduced to the idea of having their children home all of the time, and some actually kind of liked it. Sure, millions of parents counted off the undetermined days until their offspring would be returning to their regularly scheduled programming, but other families relished this time together and got a taste of what it might be like for the long term. They got to spend more time with their children in a learning environment, which is something that homeschooling families cherish. Many parents saw a frequently stressed-out child now thriving and realized that homeschooling might be a permanent solution for them. Or they saw the short length of time it took to complete schoolwork and wondered what their child was really learning or accomplishing the rest of the day in school. Still others experienced a child who was suddenly doing a great job at home but had never been a good student in the past. Or maybe they took a look at the work their student was doing and said to themselves, "Why can't I teach my child this? After all, I learned all of this in school." When it comes down to it, who knows your child better than you?

My children didn't miss a beat with school while the world imploded in March 2020. It was just life as usual, although we didn't leave the house much, except to go outside for some fresh air. As I write this chapter, I have no idea whether this tragedy will impact the number of homeschooling families there are in the world, or what long-term effects the pandemic will have on the future of homeschooling. If the COVID-19 homeschooling memes are any indication, there is a good majority of parents who are champing at the bit for their children to go back to school and finally get their time back to themselves. Conversely, there are way more than just a handful of parents that have realized that they want to continue on this journey. A recent RealClear Opinion Research poll of 2,122 registered voters found that a strong majority surveyed support school choice and 40 percent are more likely to pursue homeschooling opportunities after COVID-19 restrictions ends.[1] To all of you, I say welcome aboard. I am delighted that you are here reading this book right now. Enjoy!

introduction

"Are you insane? There's no way I would have the patience to homeschool you."

That was my go-to reply when my two extremely persistent boys first asked me to homeschool them in 2013. And the second time they inquired. And the fifty-third time they begged. Occasionally, I would give a little variation in my response; for example, "There isn't enough wine in the state of Georgia for me to homeschool you." This kept me from sounding monotonous and from boring myself. Besides, I really enjoy wine.

Even so, I started homeschooling well before the world fell apart. So, how did I choose this path? Well, my oldest son, Jesse, was nearing the end of eighth grade in public school, and we attended his pre-orientation for high school. It was a mid-February visit to the school to get a feel for the building and to meet the teachers that he might end up with, based on the courses he was interested in taking. Our first stop was the AP Biology classroom. My son was an honors science student all through middle school and sort of a phenom in all things science-, technology-, engineering-, and math-related—although, admittedly, he was not really a big fan of the M in STEM.

The classroom was filled to capacity, hot as Hades, and was standing room only, so we were pressed up against the wall for the thirty-minute presentation. It was at this moment that we started to get a bad taste in our mouths for a public school education (and I, coincidentally, started running a fever). The teacher droned on about the "two hours of homework a night" that were to be expected, the "intense curriculum," and the "killer AP exam" at the end of the year. He also seemed to be arrogantly pleased to say that only half of all students in the United States end up passing that exam and getting the college credit they worked so hard for all year. I left that room wondering why they would have two hours of homework a night. This course was equal to a college-level biology 101 course, which I had happened to take, and not once did I have two hours of homework a night. The only homework I remembered was studying for exams and writing up lab reports, and I had no problem acing my college final.

> "
> Traditional school tries to make itself a monopoly on education, but you are always free to choose your own path.
>
> LAURA KRONEN

Our next stop was the AP US Government and Politics classroom, where the teacher sternly prohibited students from taking her class if they were registering to take any other AP class during freshman year. It would be too "overwhelming" for a high school newbie to handle the course load, especially while "trying to get used to the demands of high school." As a matter of principle, we would have promptly walked out, but I was exhausted, and we had a seat this time, so we listened to her speak and viewed her PowerPoint presentation where she, multiple times, referred to the United States as the *"Untied* States." My fever was climbing, as was my tolerance level for this school.

When we got back to the car, my son looked at me and said, "Mom, I really don't want to go to this school." I had to concur. I wouldn't want to go to this school either, even though it was one of the top 100 ranked high schools in the United States and ranked solidly in the top five in our state. The drive home

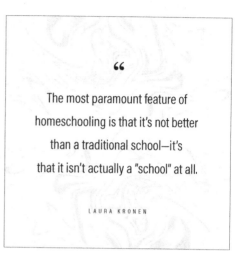

> "
> The most paramount feature of homeschooling is that it's not better than a traditional school—it's that it isn't actually a "school" at all.
>
> LAURA KRONEN

seemed to take forever, with all the traffic bottlenecking out of the school parking lot, which added to our repugnance for the evening. We finally arrived home, and I lay down on the couch with a 103-degree fever, which was diagnosed the next day as the flu and then quickly turned into pneumonia the day after that. (Thank goodness this was pre-coronavirus because I also would have been having an anxiety attack.) So, I was delirious when my son asked me for the umpteenth time if he could be homeschooled. This time I couldn't think clearly and just wanted to rest, so I said yes. He also asked me for some ridiculously expensive ant terrarium while in my feverish, hallucinogenic state, to which I also agreed. I think my kid knows how to play me. Now, here we are, three years later, willingly, blissfully, and triumphantly homeschooling with about a million ants living in a double-decker ecosystem in my dining room.

Hindsight is Twenty-Twenty

In retrospect, I wish I had started homeschooling earlier with my oldest son. Although there is nothing I can do about that now, I *can* help other people feel confident in making that decision for their family. Once I committed to homeschooling, even if it was under the influence of the influenza virus, I never looked back. I have never regretted it, not even for a minute. Is it all rainbows and sunshine? No, but most of the time it is. Is it hard work? Yes, but absolutely worth it for everyone involved. And, as a bonus, I get to learn so much along the way! I am now an excellent trivia player—in fact, I hope to be on a national knowledge-based game show very soon. It's in the works, so fingers crossed!

After agreeing to homeschool, and convalescing from three weeks of the worst illness I have ever had, I had to figure out what the heck to do. Where should I begin? How do I homeschool? I had no idea which way to turn. I didn't know anyone who homeschooled their children to even ask for advice, so I decided to approach it like I do everything else in life: I did it my way. Hey, it worked for Frank Sinatra, didn't it? My eclectic method of educating my children has led to exceptional results. Make sure to visit chapter nine for my favorite resources to help design your homeschooling curricula. It has been an invaluable learning experience that I am excited to share with anyone who has already chosen this wild and wonderful path or is considering taking the leap in the near future.

chapter one

I've Seen The Village And I Don't Want It Raising My Child

Parent-led, home-based education is an age-old traditional educational practice and is how people learned to function in the world for hundreds of years. In fact, up until the 18th century, most children received their education at home. But soon students were leaving homeschooling for the iconic one room schoolhouse and movements to standardize and secularize education were spearheaded, making homeschooling families the minority. In many cases, keeping children from a conventional school setting was considered truancy by the state and punishable in a court of law. Numerous court cases were fought in order to obtain homeschooling rights for each state.

Laws slowly evolved, and soon homeschooling was recognized as a parent's right in all fifty states, but still, the homeschooling movement seemed small, shadowy, and, frankly, a bit freaky. As a group, they seemed to be running away from the corrupt public school system, and you were as likely to find them raising chickens on a farm in the middle of nowhere, belonging to a freakish cult in a guarded compound, or half-naked in the backwoods wearing Birkenstocks and picking wildflowers. Well, maybe that's a *bit* of a stereotype, but that was the overall perception most people had of homeschooling. In the 1960s the homeschooling movement was swept aside as too quirky and too offbeat to be taken seriously and all but vanished until its resurgence in the 1970s when John Holt, an educational theorist and supporter of school reform, came on to the scene and began arguing that schools were creating an oppressive environment designed to make children compliant employees.

> "
> You do not have to have a specific reason to homeschool, and you owe an explanation to no one. You can just do it because you want to.
>
> LAURA KRONEN

But fast forward to today, and the movement is flourishing, much like the kids who are homeschooled! It represents much of what is great about American democracy and, at the same time, shows what is right and what is terribly wrong with education in America today. Homeschooling is no longer considered avant-garde and eccentric rather it borders on the mainstream in the United States with the freedom to choose being recognized and celebrated.

The National Home Education Research Institute (NHERI), an organization that measures statistics and reports trends on homeschooling, stated that home-based education just may be the fastest-growing form of education in the United States. Home-based education has also been growing around the world, including in Australia, Canada, France, Hungary, Japan, Kenya, Russia, Mexico, South Korea, Thailand, and the United Kingdom.[1] This is not shocking, as there are really compelling reasons why.

So why is homeschooling burgeoning? Whether this influx stems from a concern about the safety of the child's learning environment, dissatisfaction with academic instruction, religious beliefs, fear of political indoctrination, wanting the flexibility to school on your own terms, being able to travel the world for hands-on education, or the desire to focus on family relationships, you are definitely not alone in your reasons for exploring the idea of homeschooling.

Here are the top thirteen reasons for considering a home-based education for your children.

1. SAFETY

You just have to listen to the news or scroll through social media to learn about yet another horrifying school shooting. Fearing for your child's safety when they leave the house just to get an education is a dreadful feeling. Many schools now have armed guards patrolling the halls, metal detectors at the entrances, and locked doors that only school personnel can open; all are definitely deterrents to mass shooters but sound more like a four-year asylum for teenagers or a jail than an actual school. (My children always equated their public school experience to "being incarcerated.")

2. VIOLENCE

Shootings aren't the only form of violence that is happening at schools across the world. Bullying is occurring on every campus and in every age group, and is far more common than you are even aware of. According to StopBullying.gov, bullying is defined as "unwanted, aggressive behavior [i.e., behavior that is intentional and mean] among school-aged children that involves a real or perceived power imbalance."[2] This behavior is repeated over time or has the potential to be repeated, and both kids who are bullied and kids who bully others may have serious, lasting problems. Although supposedly not tolerated by schools, bullying is still happening, and it is ruining some children's educations and lives. Some people consider bullying "a part of growing up" or "kids being kids," but I don't. It doesn't build character. It increases vulnerability, and these children really suffer.

Sadly, many school-aged children are exposed to bullying in some form due to the unequal balance of power and influence that is so common in youth relationships and peer groups. In fact, StopBullying.gov reports that as many as one in every three school-aged children say they have been bullied in school. Research shows that bullying and harassment in schools increases in late childhood and peaks in early adolescence, specifically during middle school, and typically takes place in unstructured settings such as the cafeteria, hallways, the bathroom, physical education, and the playground during recess. Forms of bullying range from name-calling to teasing, spreading rumors or lies, physical violence, making threats, attacking someone verbally, stealing belongings, sexual comments or obscene gestures, excluding someone from a group on purpose, and of course, the awful, self-esteem-stealing social media harassment.[3]

Fortunately, there are actions that students and school staff can take to prevent bullying and harassment and to create a more positive school climate. But it takes consistent and united action by everyone—students, staff, administrators, and parents. Unfortunately, there is often a disconnect between a young person's experience of bullying and what adults perceive. Children are tragically going to the furthest extremes when bullying becomes too much for them to handle. More research from StopBullying.gov indicates that persistent bullying can lead to or worsen feelings of isolation, rejection, exclusion, and despair, as well as depression and anxiety, and can contribute to suicidal behavior.

Bullying is one reason to consider or to justify homeschooling your children. Rampant drug use in schools is another.

3. SUBSTANCE ABUSE

Despite popular community and school programs that condemn the use and abuse of vaping, alcohol, and drugs, the Centers for Disease Control (CDC) report that teen drug use is on the rise. The percentage of America's middle school and high school students who use alcohol and marijuana continues to increase, along with students' use of several other categories of drugs, including prescription painkillers and inhalants. At the same time, anti-drug attitudes among teenagers have deteriorated.[4]

As marijuana is legalized in some states and the perceived harm of drugs dwindles, teens will encounter drugs and alcohol on a more regular basis in schools. The fear is real that the harmful patterns of teen substance abuse will continue to escalate as well. This isn't to say that homeschooled kids are immune to these problems, but the less you put your child into situations where kids are doing drugs and places where drugs are very accessible, the less likely your child will be to encounter the peer pressure to try them. With homeschooling, you can provide guided and reasoned social interactions for your children and have a sound knowledge of who makes up their circle of friends.

4. TO GET A HIGHER QUALITY EDUCATION AT HOME

No one knows your child better than you, and you have a vested interest in your own child's development and success. Public school teachers attend "professional development" workshops every so often to discover new information on how children learn, but research on education topics can be found online for free, and you can access this information whenever you want. That's why even homeschooling parents who don't have teaching degrees can be familiar with the latest news on how to be a better teacher.

Homeschooling gives parents more control over what their kids are learning. There is a strong belief that the traditional school curriculum is not providing the right knowledge and skills for children. A recent college and career readiness survey conducted by YouthTruth reported that less than half of high school students feel academically ready for college and that college professors believe students are less prepared for college work as well.[5] When I pulled my oldest son from public school, he was entering his first year of high school, and I was confident that I would be able to give him a better education than he was getting in one of the top high schools in Georgia. It would take some research, time, and effort on my part, but I committed to making it work, and the fruits of my labor have already paid off tenfold.

With crowded classrooms and fewer resources, it is more difficult for teachers to provide one-on-one instruction to students. However, with a home-based education, parents can either use a state-approved curriculum and supplement it by delivering personalized instruction that is often missing in today's public schools or they can completely reinvent the wheel and develop their own curriculum that will challenge and excite their child, which is what I did. Parents can spend as little time or as much time as needed on each subject to ensure their children are learning the intended material and feel confident they have conquered the course lessons.

"
There is no school better than a loving and encouraging home.

LAURA KRONEN

According to Business Insider, homeschooled children tend to score better on state and federal standardized tests and another recent article by NHERI stated that home-educated kids typically score 15 to 30 percentage points above public school students on standardized academic achievement tests. (The public school average is in the fiftieth percentile.)[6] In fact, the results are even better for black homeschooled students, according to a study published in the *Journal of School Choice* regarding African American homeschooling motivations and academic achievement. The research found that black homeschool students score 23 to 42 percentage points higher than black students in public schools.[7] Home-educated students also typically score above average on SAT and ACT tests that colleges consider for admission.[8] All of these increases are true regardless of parents' income, level of education, or if they have any experience teaching.

5. RELIGIOUS BELIEFS

Contrary to popular opinion, religion is not the sole reason people choose to homeschool their kids. Still, it does play a part in many families' decisions to remove their children from a traditional classroom setting. Some people want their children to be raised in a more moral or religious environment than they might find in a conventional school setting. These homeschooling families are hoping that more time with their kids will help give them the foundation they need to keep their faith in God as an adult.

Each generation in America appears to be less religious than the last. This means many individuals are not keeping their parents' religion when they grow up. As a result, the United States has slowly become more and more secular over the years. Research shows that many of the people who reject their parents' religion as adults have grown up in an environment that it's important to think for themselves and find their own moral compass. They have a do-it yourself attitude towards religion and most everything and have rejected traditional institutions.[9]

According to the research, there are more significant factors that determine a person's religion than whether or not they were homeschooled. "A person who was raised in a nurturing, loving environment is more likely to stick with their parents' religious beliefs than those who didn't feel loved or spend as much time with their parents," states the nondenominational Universal Life Church. "Another important factor is how devoted the parents are to their religion. For example, families who attend church regularly, pray together regularly, and stay involved in their religious community will more likely raise children who stay with their religion than people who don't."[10]

6. TO AVOID RACISM

A 2012 report in the *Journal of Black Studies* surveyed black homeschooling families from around the country and found that most chose to educate their children at home, at least in part to avoid school-related racism.[11] A typical public school curriculum begins African American history with slavery and ends it with the civil rights movement. Black parents who choose to homeschool will often teach a more comprehensive view of African history by including a more detailed description of ancient African civilizations and accounts of successful African people throughout history. Children can build their sense of racial pride and self-esteem more readily when exposed to more information. But it isn't just African American families who feel that way. Many other cultures want to give their children an international perspective of the world and also include more instruction from their own culture and history.

7. VACCINATIONS

I wasn't sure I even wanted to broach this topic, but some families do choose to homeschool their children rather than submit to state requirements that their children be vaccinated. A variety of factors are at play: religious and philosophical beliefs, freedom and individualism, misinformation about risk, and over-perception of risk. The social media term for these advocates is "anti-vaxxers." According to an article in the *Washington Post*, the percentage of US children who have not received any vaccine has quadrupled since 2001.[12] The World Health Organization (WHO) insists that vaccines are actually very safe, and most adverse effects are minor and temporary, like a sore arm or a mild fever.[13] The rewards far outweigh the risks. Even one or two serious adverse effects in a million doses of vaccine cannot be warranted if there is no benefit from the vaccination. If there were no vaccines, there would be many more cases of disease and, consequently, more severe side effects and more deaths. The latest global pandemic is proof positive of this. The CDC states that, "Although vaccines have dramatically reduced the number of people who get infectious diseases and the complications these diseases produce, the viruses and bacteria that cause vaccine-preventable diseases and death still exist. Without vaccines, epidemics of vaccine-preventable diseases would return."[14]

There are arguments both for and against vaccinations, and arming yourself with as much research as possible is the best way to make an educated and responsible decision. But, for the record, this was not one of my reasons for homeschooling my children. They have all of their vaccinations and even get the flu shot every year.

8. POLITICS

There is no denying that our left-leaning public education system is breeding a certain standard of electorate, and democratic views are primarily what our children are exposed to daily as they journey through their dozen or so years of public school education. Many times the liberal messages have good intentions but sometimes they come across as unfair and unbalanced.

My child experienced this full-on while attending public school during an election year. His eighth-grade debate class teacher assigned the students to watch all of the Democratic primary debates, write about the candidates, and discuss them ad nauseam in class the next day. This would have

> **"**
>
> People should have the freedom to choose the educational experience they want for their children.
>
> LAURA KRONEN

been absolutely fine by me if she also assigned them to watch the Republican debates, but she didn't. Not a single one. I was outraged by this blunt bias and asked for a meeting with the principal and the teacher to find out how they can get away with this type of narrow-minded mentality. It was no surprise that I was told in no uncertain terms that my opinion has zero impact on a class syllabus or assignments and to leave the teaching to the professionals. My head almost exploded in that conference room that day, and I immediately yanked my kid out of the class.

After researching this further, I found evidence that suggests why that happened. The Pacific Research Institute recently published an extensive chart from Verdant Labs on the average political affiliations of various professions. Among the results they found that among English teachers, there are 97 Democrats for every three Republicans, with the proportion being even more one-sided among health teachers, with 99 Democrats for every one Republican. While there are slightly more Republicans among math and science teachers, among high school teachers overall, there are 87 Democrats for every 13 Republicans.[15]

I do not want my child to be fed an agenda. I want him to decide for himself what works for his beliefs and future. To do that, you need exposure to all of the information, not just what one person wants to push on you. Luckily both of my children are independents, and through homeschooling, they have learned to think for themselves.

9. FLEXIBILITY

Homeschooling allows you to be the master of your own time. It sounds appealing, doesn't it? Shouldn't we all be able to plan according to our wants and needs and not according to what the school district you reside in demands from you? Scheduling appointments for doctor visits, voice lessons, vacations, and even haircuts are so much easier when you do not have to work around traditional school hours and jockey for spots against the other school kids. The same goes for creating your own work schedule if you choose to work outside the home. No more worrying about getting home early for the bus on teacher workdays or scrambling for childcare on holidays that you do not get off work for. Now you can plan according to your own timetable.

Flexibility is also vital when you have a child who has a deep desire to focus on a specific skill. Many kids might argue that playing video games falls under this category, but what I am referring to is a child who dreams of being a professional actor, artist, dancer, musician, or athlete. Taking these aspirations seriously requires intense training that goes way past what an after-school club can offer. Making your own school timetable allows plenty of hours for lessons, coaching, instruction, rehearsals, and auditions. When you think about it, shouldn't school allow every kid to focus on what they love and want to do with their lives "when they grow up"? I'm not saying math is not essential—everything in life has a math component, from cooking to electronics—and language arts and writing courses are definitely non-negotiable. Still, there are certain electives, and respective busy work that goes along with them, that many career-focused students can live without. Spending time honing a craft, meanwhile, is time well spent.

10. TRAVEL

The world is our classroom. As homeschoolers, we can go wherever and whenever we want. You know those fabulous off-season rates? We get to take advantage of them. Someone told me the other day that their kids love the atmosphere of being in Disney when it is crowded. Seriously? What kid wants to stand in line for hours at a time? What parent wants to hear the constant complaints of how hot it is and how their child can't stand up anymore?

Traveling (and not just to Disney) is a beautiful way to learn about the world. We not only study different places and cultures, but we get to visit them as well. Best field trips ever! At the time my son was reading Shakespeare's *Romeo and Juliet,* we had the opportunity to visit Verona, Italy, the setting of the play, which features the two star-crossed lovers from rival families. Being able to immerse ourselves in the play while walking through the very village Shakespeare wrote of, made unrhymed iambic pentameter way more interesting to all of us.

Not all field trips are as amazing as that, but I try to expose my kids to as many different cultural experiences as possible. Every month we go somewhere different, whether it be to a different city to learn firsthand about its history and culture (and its food!) or to a local museum or cultural event, the ability to make learning thought-provoking and intriguing is priceless. Why keep your children hidden away in school when they could be learning in the ever-changing, bright, and stimulating real world?

11. SLEEP

Homeschooled students get more sleep than their peers who attend public schools. Studies from National Jewish Health found that homeschool students average more than ninety minutes more sleep per night than their friends who need to make it to school by the first period.[16] Right now, the typical public school system is set up so that the very youngest children, who are naturally awake very early in the morning, start school the latest. Our adolescents, who need to sleep the most and who stay up the latest, are being asked to wake up and go to school

at a time when their brains should still physiologically be asleep. According to the National Sleep Foundation, adolescents need nine hours of sleep a night, and if they're only getting seven hours on average, by the end of the school week, they are a full ten hours of sleep behind schedule.[17] That impacts every aspect of functioning at the highest level.

That cumulative sleep deprivation adds up and has real ramifications. The ability to learn, concentrate, and pay attention is diminished when you haven't had enough sleep. But beyond that, a lack of sleep can also impact a teenager's mood and their ability to drive early in the morning.

You might say, "If your teenager needs more sleep, why not just send them to bed earlier?" But, c'mon, we all know it's not that simple. We can coax our little ones to sleep with rituals and rules, but teenagers are a little harder to read fairy tales to in the hopes that they fall into a blissful slumber. What's more, if you've got two hours of homework each night just in one subject (e.g., AP Bio), you don't have the ability to go to bed early—even if you desperately want to. It has been reported in the journal *Behavioral Sleep Medicine* that melatonin, the hormone that helps regulate our sleep, shifts ahead by about two hours during puberty.[18] So, even if they wanted to get to sleep earlier, teenagers are battling biological changes in their bodies that are nearly impossible to overcome.

The logical solution is to let them sleep later. The added benefit of a homeschooling schedule is that you have just removed the stress of waking up a child who doesn't want to be woken up and eliminating that battle every morning. By no means do I think homeschooled kids should sleep in as late as they want, but I do believe that nine o'clock is a reasonable start time to the day.

Another benefit is that parents get more sleep and less stress too! Now we don't have to get up early to meet a bus, prepare lunches, or get in a carpool lane. Our mornings are great times together to snuggle with our children, have a relaxing breakfast, and talk about our plans for the day. No more "Hurry up and get dressed, brush your teeth, and eat breakfast, or you'll be late for school!" No more leaving things at home and having to run back up to school with the sheet of homework that your child thought they put in their backpack (but actually left on the kitchen counter) or with their lunch that they forgot on the bus so that they are not forced to eat the revolting cafeteria food. As I am writing this, I realize I could dedicate an entire chapter to cafeteria food as the sole reason to homeschool, but there are bigger fish to fry. Speaking of which, never eat the cafeteria fish!

12. TO HELP A CHILD WHO NEEDS MORE ATTENTION

While every child is unique and has specific needs, some students learn differently than others. Students with special needs may have learning challenges, or they may work on a level that is different from their peers. Hundreds of thousands of children have learning concerns such as dyslexia, dysgraphia, ADD, ADHD, autism, or hearing or vision loss. Some children can even have severe allergies or an autoimmune disease that causes them to miss school frequently. Many times these types of students perform dramatically better in the home environment as compared to the traditional classroom.

The homeschool environment provides all the accommodations a student might need to help them learn best. Students with handwriting issues can use a keyboard instead of being forced to write. Children who have distraction issues can use devices such as stress balls or fidget toys to help them pay attention, or they can even move around the room while learning. Children who have sensory challenges can perform extraordinarily well in a home environment with surroundings that help them stay calm, including lighting adjustments, soft rugs, comfortable clothing, and cozy chairs. Children who need additional testing time to do well on tests can be afforded at that time. Sometimes this extra time can make all the difference in the quality of a student's work.

13. FOSTER GREAT RELATIONSHIPS WITH FAMILY

The very best reason for homeschooling is to create lasting and happy relationships with your children. Our family spends the best hours of each day together. Before, I was giving my kids away during their best hours, when they were rested and happy, and then getting them back when they were tired, grumpy, and hungry. I dreaded each evening, when the constant homework battle never seemed to end and my job was to push them through that, plus all of their extracurriculars. Now, we have our happy time together each day and enjoy being in each other's company.

Regardless of your *why*, homeschooling is increasing by

large numbers. According to NHERI, there are over 2.5 million homeschooled students in the United States, and the homeschool population is continuing to grow at an estimated 2 to 8 percent per annum over the past few years.[19] It is the fastest-growing form of education in the United States. Because of these statistics, some states are trying to ban and restrict homeschooling, which makes me want to do it even more! I'm a rebel like that. Banning free thinking is the ultimate form of control, and the very last thing I would want is for my children to exist in a groupthink world where individuality is blotted out.

Agreeing with a little bit of many of these reasons is a good reason to homeschool, not just because of one on its own. Do not homeschool if you can't handle the thought of being away from your child or if you are scared of what might happen to them in school. That is homeschooling in fear, and it will have a trickle-down effect on your child. And don't homeschool out of guilt or comparison to someone else because you will never live up to them. There is no "typical homeschooler." There are endless types of personalities with different belief systems, cultures, races, and backgrounds with many combinations of reasons to homeschool. No matter who you are, what you think, or where you live, you will fit in.

chapter two

Life Is All About Choices

When it comes to the education of your children, you want to make sure that you provide them with the best possible opportunities, ultimately producing a competent, educated young adult who is prepared for the real world. Generally speaking, there are three choices of educational systems to make that happen: public school, private school, and home school.

For many people, private school is out of their budget. While a private education might be better than a public one, it can be costly. Depending on the school, it can cost (tens of) thousands of dollars per year. That prices private school right out of most people's pocketbooks.

Public schooling is free, and each child is guaranteed to receive an education. There are public schools everywhere, usually with free transportation provided, so you don't have to participate in any of the education processes aside from getting your child out to the bus stop on time. But as with most things in life, you get what you pay for. If it's for free, there is a chance that it is probably not your best option. I'm not sure if you have ever thought of it that way or if you just assumed that because "everyone did it," it was the best or only possibility.

Public School Problems

Once upon a time, America created a public education system that was the envy of the modern world, producing highly educated high school and college graduates. It was upon this that the American middle class was built. But then, sometime around the 1970s, America lost its way. Our schools began to crumble, and our test scores and graduation rates fell. Public schools started failing our system. Currently, American students can't keep up with the students in other countries, and the average US fourth grader doesn't even have the most basic proficiency in science, reading, or history.[1] So, what happened?

People typically assume that the problem with the public education system is a lack of funding, but this is not fundamentally the case. The foundation that the system is built on is cracked, and until these issues are repaired, nothing will solve the problem. You see, the public school system is not held responsible for the undereducated students it spits out. Schools can flat-out ignore parents (it's happened to me countless times) as well as anyone else they do not receive funding from.

And what if a school is chock-full of bad teachers? My children had quite a few. What do you think happens to those educators? That's right. Absolutely nothing. They keep their job, they keep on people-shaping with their programmed information, and the public school stays in business. Customer satisfaction is not a concern in the public education business, especially when the customers are uneducated kids who won't realize they got the short end of the stick until they enter college or the workforce and find that they can't keep up. Accountability is something that is lacking in our society and our school systems.

Despite higher-than-average per-pupil expenditures, public-educated students in the US are seriously lagging behind public-educated students in other countries.[2] According to The Census Bureau, public schools receive an average of $11,762 per pupil—twice the average amount spent per student at private and charter schools. Some areas, like the District of Columbia, spend more than $19,159 per public-educated pupil.[3] Where is the money going? Does anybody know or care? If I was given that much cash to educate my child, you can bet that they would have the very best of everything! But that is not the case in our schools, not even close. Those who run our schools have no personal risk or vested interest to cut costs or increase revenue. When a school produces bad results or spends all of its money, that school usually just receives even more funding—again, with no accountability for where it is going aside from a generic line item on a budget.

Political agendas are another problem within schools. Public schools are not required to answer to parents. Still, they do need to take into account the words of politicians and school boards—all of whom have their political agendas—hence the reason my son's debate teacher was pushing the liberal agenda and insisting that her students not educate themselves on any other political party. These agendas are weakening the entire framework of education. Schools and teachers are forced to deal with supposedly brilliant plans and programs thought up by local, state, and federal governments, and then the taxpayers are expected to foot the bill to put the ideas into motion.

Bureaucracies spend a lot of time discussing education without ever discussing learning. We separate church and state, so why not school and state? By shutting out the self-concerned politicians and giving power to the parents and teachers, real accountability may come about.

Another reason for our failing schools is that they take on a one-size-fits-all prescription for education. Gifted students often take the same types of classes as students who need more emotional and academic support. In eighth grade, my son was in a regular level algebra class and even though he hated math (albeit he loves it now that he is homeschooled), begged me to get him placed in an honors class because many students at the regular level were disrespectful to their teacher and peers. So much of the time in the classroom was dedicated to discipline instead of learning.

In rural areas, there are rarely AP courses or other course options that will allow those gifted students to shine. Good teachers aren't given a chance to show what they are made of and teach children how to think because they are forced to follow the standardized-testing lesson plans that have been laid out for them. The modern-day public school system is extremely problematic in that it discards millions of average to even extremely bright children as failures, and in the end, everyone loses. The entire education system is an intricate system meant to filter out the youth who think for themselves, who are too independent, and who are not submissive enough. These types of people destroy the institutions.

What about class sizes? Typically, class sizes in public schools remain smaller, relatively speaking, in the early years, from kindergarten through about third grade. You might have one teacher to every twenty-five students. At that point, classes gradually grow in accordance with the students' age and ability to work independently. By the time high school comes around, classrooms are packed with students, and individualized attention no longer exists. Your child is basically a number, part of a ratio that could be 1:35 in every class. And each teacher has a multitude of classes.

"

Once you start homeschooling, the quest for knowledge becomes addictive.

LAURA KRONEN

Additionally, compulsory education is geared to teach the average student. That means that the gifted students are bored, and the kids who are struggling keep getting left further and further behind. That also means that your child doesn't get the help that they need when they need it.

Do the Pros Outweigh the Cons?

Let's look at the positive attributes of public schooling, though. When it comes down to it, the cost of a public education can't be beaten. Although some parents might complain about the added expense of school supplies and expenses associated with participation in clubs and sports, these schools are still much more budget-conscious than private schools. Depending on where you live, private schools can average around $10,000 per year, while the average cost for a boarding school is approximately $35,000 annually. Besides, private schools get much of their funding through donations, which could mean that parents of students may have to invest time and money in fundraising events each year. Of course, public schools also participate in fundraisers, but the majority of funding still comes from federal, state, and local government sources.

Public schools also must provide access to education for every child in a community. By law, public schools cannot turn students away for any reason, including academic performance, income level, or disability. This ensures that every student in the same area will have equal educational opportunities regardless of their personal or financial situation. Education is the great equalizer for society, and the availability of education for all is a crucial benefit these institutions offer.

Because public schools admit all children in the community, students are more likely to be exposed to students from different backgrounds, cultures, and income levels. They are also likely to be in classrooms with other students that don't think, act, or look exactly like them. They may interact with students that have mental and/or physical disabilities. This diversity of the student body can be a valuable learning experience in itself for every child. It is crucial, after all, that our children know how to interact with all different types of people in society.

In addition to choices in the classroom, students in public schools often have many prospects for extracurricular activities. This can be considered very appealing to some, but to some anti-public schoolers, they can seem like just another scrupulously designed social construct. From athletics to music, theater, and science clubs, most schools offer a variety of choices to keep students learning and excelling in the areas they are most interested in. If your child aspires to play pro football one day, chances are he would have to participate on more than just a club-level football team to get the experience needed to ultimately be recruited for college-level play. If your public school does not offer homeschoolers the option to play on a team (some states and counties forbid it), then the best option for your son (or daughter—hey, if a woman wants to get tackled on the field, that's her choice—all hail women's lib!) is to be given that opportunity in public school.

By law, public schools are also required to provide services such as transportation to and from school. Reduced-price lunches and academic assistance are also services provided to students who qualify. Public schools are also required to have special education teachers and specialists for students who require such help. Private schools may not offer these services because they are not required to admit students that meet these needs. If you choose to homeschool, all of this is irrelevant, but it is good to be able to weigh all the pros versus the cons.

Certification is another positive aspect of public schools, although sometimes I wonder how some of these teachers passed their tests. While there is no certification requirement to homeschool your child, public school teachers are required to be certified by the state. Certification also requires continuing education and renewal of credentials. Private schools do not have this obligation, which means parents don't always know the level of training fulfilled by their child's teacher. Some private schools might not even require teachers to have a degree at all to work in the classroom.

Public schools are also held accountable by the state for their academic performance. While many have lamented that this has led to a profuse amount of unnecessary standardized testing, public schools do at least have a higher power that they must respond to. This leads to the regulation and management of failing schools much more quickly than if the schools did not have such accountability.

Standardized testing is a point of contention for homeschoolers. Some families do not believe in them, but I encourage (coerce) my children to take them as benchmarks for how well we are doing. (I say "we" because homeschooling is a collaborative effort!) Besides, most colleges require SAT or ACT scores for admission. Much more on standardized testing to come! But if your child does not plan on attending college or is opting for a technical career, then standardized testing isn't a priority. According to Public School Review, students in public schools score comparably on standardized tests to students in private schools. While some public schools turn up relatively poor results, those results are often found in areas with high poverty rates.[4] When comparing apples to apples in terms of student demographics, public schools are right up there with other types of schools.

There are benefits to a public school education. However,

> "
> Life will never introduce something
> to you that you will not
> be able to figure out.
> You are ready.
> You can do this.
>
> LAURA KRONEN

this education system has the best propaganda programming in the world, making you believe that you need it, so it is no wonder that the majority of students and their parents are still making their local public school their first choice for education. But for those who believe the force-feeding of their children should not be an option anymore, or who are irritated by passionless public education, homeschooling is a compelling consideration. Changing times call for changing minds.

The Homeschool Alternative

Homeschooling is another option for education, and undoubtedly the reason you are here. Homeschooled kids account for roughly 3 to 4 percent of school-aged children in the United States.[5] That is a number equivalent to those attending charter schools and higher than those attending parochial schools. To touch just the tippy-top of the iceberg, there are a lot of reasons for this. One is because homeschooled children get the individualized education that parents want them to. Their schooling is geared around the child and will work toward their strengths and help them with their weaknesses. Parents get to spend a lot of time at home with their children, so while their offspring are being educated, they are also getting to bond with them. The gifted kids get to work at the speed they want, while the kids who are struggling are able to spend all the time they need to get caught up and stay caught up.

As favorable as homeschooling is—and you will soon behold the myriad of reasons for that—it wouldn't be fair if I didn't mention the drawbacks. One is that your kids won't always be around a bunch of other kids, so they won't have that same level of socialization, which could be a negative. But you can prevent that. There is also some cost associated with homeschooling, mostly to buy the supplies that are needed, but they average about $500 to $1,500 a year, allowing you to find the curriculum plan that works the best for your child.

Of the endless reasons to homeschool, there are plenty of people that still will knock it. A recent study reported in *Harvard Magazine* sees risks in homeschooling children and is recommending a ban on the practice, insisting it "violates children's rights to a meaningful education."[6] One concern the study presented is that people who do not have a quality education and who might not even be able to read and write can homeschool their children. While I am against a regulatory body for my homeschooling methods, I would agree with the last statement. It goes back to what I said earlier: you should be striving to give your child the best possible education. If you are not capable of doing that, your child should be in a public or private school. Swallow your pride.

Another concern pointed out by *Harvard Magazine* is that teachers are required to alert the authorities when it comes time to report evidence of child abuse or neglect.[7] They make up the most significant percentage of people who report to Child Protective Services (CPS). Currently, there is no requirement for homeschool parents to be checked for prior reports of child abuse. I also agree, in this specific instance, that homeschooling should be monitored. I also think if you touch your child in an abusive manner, you should have your limbs cut off one by one—just so you are clear where I stand.

A paper published recently in the *Arizona Law Review* lists an array of reasons parents choose homeschooling. Some find local schools lacking or want to protect their child from bullying. Others do it to give their children the flexibility to pursue sports or other activities at a high level. But surveys of homeschoolers show that a majority of such families—by some estimates, up to 90 percent—are driven by conservative Christian beliefs, and seek to remove their children from mainstream culture. It was also stated that some of these parents have "extreme religious ideologies" and question science and promote female subservience.[8] While I'm sure this exists, I do not know anyone within any of the homeschool communities that I have encountered that fits this description. While I am sure there are crazies in every corner of society, I beg to differ on that percentage. *Ninety*? Nope. Plus, how do you find that out? In a survey sent to homeschooling families? Give me a break. That is sensationalism at its finest.

> "
> Every moment of every day can be a learning moment. Everyday experiences that help children learn about the world they live in is learning.
>
> LAURA KRONEN

In most situations, homeschooling is justified and effective. If parents are motivated and capable of giving their children an education that's of a higher quality than what is available in public schools, then homeschooling is the right option. So whether it comes down to public school, private school, or homeschool, a lot of the decision comes down to what will work best for you and your kids. Not all kids will work well with homeschool, and not all parents are cut out for homeschooling.

Legal Jargon

At this point, I know why you are here, and I don't think I have to sell you on homeschooling. You are seriously interested in getting started, and are probably excited about jumping right in. But there are some initial steps you need to take. By now, you realize that homeschooling is legal throughout the United States. Still, each state is free to create its legal structure for home education, so one state's homeschooling laws may look very different from another's.

No matter where you live, you can withdraw your child from public school whenever you want, even midyear, but there are steps you need to follow. Some states are highly regulated, like Massachusetts, New York, Pennsylvania, Rhode Island, and Vermont, while others place few restrictions on homeschooling families. The Homeschool Legal Defense Association (hslda.org/legal) maintains an up-to-date database on the homeschooling laws in all fifty states, and this should be your first stop. Whether you consider your state's homeschooling laws restrictive or lenient, it is essential to make sure you understand what is required of you and remain compliant. So go check that out, and I'll be waiting right here for you.

chapter three

Like Frank Sinatra,
I Did It My Way!

When it comes to homeschooling, we are doing school for our children our way. Research studies show that, compared to kids in traditional schools, homeschooled kids grow up with stronger friendships, better relationships with their parents and adults, greater empathy for people and situations, and a greater sense of social responsibility.[1] We homeschool to prepare our children for a world that is nothing like traditional school. Life has a million pathways, and the universe appreciates energy, differences, independence, and the idiosyncrasies of singularity.

A Little About Me

Growing up, I was never homeschooled. I do not think that thought ever crossed my parents' minds. There were five of us kids (four of them boys), and unquestionably, my mom needed the break when we left for school in the morning. And that is OK. Homeschooling is absolutely not for everyone. Plus, it was a completely different world back then. My generation was not fearful of school shootings; bullying was no more than a heated disagreement, maybe with an accompanying push or shove, before we were all blithesome friends again; and social media was (thankfully) nonexistent. I really loved school when I was growing up.

I was the captain of the cheerleaders, on the student council, and in the National Honor Society, among so many other extracurriculars. I couldn't even wait for summer to be over so I could go back to my friends and all my activities. I also enjoyed doing homework at night. So why in the world would I ever homeschool my kids? I sometimes wonder that myself, and that's a question I get asked a lot. I get a lot of "Better you than me" and the occasional "How can you be around your kids that much?" Well, truth be told, I love being around my kids. They are young for just a short time. I try to spend as much time with them as possible, and I enjoy their company. They have so many things they want to talk about and experience, and I can make sure their voices aren't silenced, which public school has an insidious way of doing.

There's No Place Like Home for the Holidays

Public schools also squelch the celebration of most holidays, which was the very first thing that rubbed me the wrong way about the school system. I was the "room mom" when my kids were in public elementary school. Every year, I had to put together a "winter-themed" party that could not have anything symbolic of personal beliefs. Santa Claus, reindeer, trees, stars, menorahs—they were all forbidden. However, I was always the

mom who broke the rules and did what I thought the kids would enjoy. These holiday icons are secular symbols of fun and festivity during the season. If that meant decorating tree cookies with frosting and M&M's and making stained-glass ornaments, or pasting together googly-eyed, pom-pom-nosed, construction paper reindeers, then so be it! I wasn't trying to drag kids into a religious cult, I was allowing them to have fun! The kids were so bored year after year of penguin-, snowflake-, and snowmen- (*yawn*) themed parties, and frankly, so was I. So I did what I wanted to do; I'm a rebel like that. "Ask for forgiveness later" is my motto. No one ever reported me, but I did see other room moms peeking in my room, longingly wishing that they had the nerve to buck the system.

Other forbidden holidays included Halloween, St. Patrick's Day, and Easter. Halloween was replaced with a "storybook parade," though. *Yawn again.* Case in point: Schools are removing every bit of culture and tradition from our children today. As depressing as it was, the eradication of holidays was not even close to being a deciding factor for me in making the leap to homeschool my boys, but many things were.

My Why

The core idea of homeschooling is the concept that kids get to learn at the speed, and in the style, most appropriate for them. Homeschooling parents are in the best position possible to know and provide the right kind of instruction for their child. Homeschooling allows us to enrich our children's strengths and supplement their weaknesses. Their education moves as fast or as slow as needed for any particular subject. They are not pigeonholed and tracked as gifted, average, or special needs.

Without a formal curriculum to guide their education, homeschoolers get the chance to explore a range of topics that

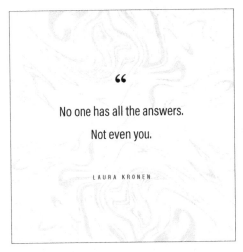

> "
>
> No one has all the answers.
> Not even you.
>
> LAURA KRONEN

might not be generally offered until high school or college. They can study astronomy in fourth grade or economics in eighth grade. My youngest son loves music, so one of his semesters of language arts was focusing solely on music lyrics and the literary elements found within them. He learned so much because he enjoyed what he was doing. This is just one example of how you can tailor what your child is learning to their interests to make them love learning even more! While many homeschool families do teach math, science, social studies, and language arts, education is by no means limited just to those subjects. Some parents are capable enough to pass on vast amounts of knowledge themselves, but many parents rely on approved online learning platforms, videos, and workbooks, which is perfectly permissible and appropriate.

Homeschoolers don't have to deal with all the drawbacks of being around kids in a septic school environment. Although some might argue the negative elements of public school are actually good for toughening kids up, kids who are bullied more often have negative educational outcomes and do worse in class. Why do we need to have other kids be mean and nasty to our children to toughen them up? In fact, why do we want kids to be "tough" at all? Homeschooled kids are able to learn in a more family-oriented and growth-oriented environment. I'll take my sweet, humble, and loving kids any day of the week over a smart-mouthed kid who has been "toughened up."

Contrary to the name, homeschooling takes place in an actual home only a fraction of the time. A great deal of instruction happens in museums, nature centers, and really anywhere you want to go. These life experiences cultivate a trait of open-mindedness and cultural awareness. Since kids spend more time around adults in the real world, they seldom come to view school as separate from their "real lives" and instead as just an *extension* of who they are. They are continually learning.

Our public education system is full of rules: Be punctual. Report to school and class on time. In case of absence, parents must call the school on the morning of the absence and then notify the teacher in writing upon the student's return to school. Students must maintain order when moving to different areas of the building. Do not run. Do not have cell phones, yo-yos, pets, skateboards, money, toys, or gum in your knapsack or on your person. Ask permission to talk or go to the bathroom. Remain within school boundaries at all times. Do not climb trees or gates or railings. Leave the premises immediately after your school responsibilities are over. Do not buy or sell personal items. Dress in a specific way. But kids who are just given rules without learning about principles become pretty masterful at finding the loopholes in the laws, hiding their noncompliance, and even worse, lying about it. These are the skills they are bringing into their adulthood.

Homeschooling also makes sense from an achievement point of view. According to a recent article in *Business Insider*, it is proven that homeschooled children tend to do better on standardized tests, stick around longer in college, and do better once they're enrolled.[2] And *US News* and *World Report* stated that the proportion of homeschoolers who graduated from college was about 67 percent, while among public school students, it was 58 percent.[3] That is a notable difference. Students from Catholic and private schools fell even lower in college graduation rates, with 54 and 51 percent of kids, respectively, completing all four years. These are not good percentages when you consider how much college costs!

My kids were slated for the top high schools in Georgia, among the top in the entire nation, but my choice to homeschool wasn't based on the ranking or the availability of good schools. Taking my children's education into my own hands lets me (and them) choose what they are learning and control the influences around them. I also have the unique privilege of learning and relearning *with* my kids. I minored in Spanish in college and haven't used it since then, except on a trip to Cancun. Now it is all coming back to me as I teach my boys a language. Guess it's finally coming in handy! At this point, I know more about our government, biology, psychology, space, history, physics, art, and philosophy than I had ever learned in college.

Another bonus of being at the helm of our academic scheduling is that my kids get to sleep later in the morning. Kids need sleep! And so do I because I am a night owl and a morning person and an afternoon person, so when I do actually sleep, I *need* it! Our day begins peacefully without having to run for the bus or pack lunches. That stress is gone. I always thought it was preposterous that my kindergartner had to be at the bus stop at 7:10 a.m. Who decided that the youngest kids, who require the most sleep, should begin school the earliest? We start school after breakfast, usually around nine or nine thirty; we work until about twelve thirty and eat lunch; and then start up again and work until about four. I'm a work- from-home mom and a life coach, consult for a few companies, work on my entrepreneurial ventures, and write books in between it all. I promise you that you will

> "
> Homeschooled kids don't miss out on anything. Their schooling and life just look a little different from everyone else's. What fun is life if everyone has the same experience?
>
> LAURA KRONEN

be able to find the time once you discover your rhythm. More on that to come later.

So overall, my children have six to seven hours of vigorous, focused schoolwork per day. While a traditional school might go for seven or eight hours, the learning time is significantly less when you add in transferring between classes and all of the wasted time that occurs in classrooms, waiting on late teachers, contending with problem students, and preparing for weeks of standardized testing.

Teaching for *your* child means being able to change the day's direction on a dime. You can adapt your teaching style daily if that is what your child needs to learn best. If my son wakes up one morning and decides that he wants to be a doctor, we can put our regularly scheduled plan on hold and focus on topics like biology and chemistry for a few hours. We can research how to take someone's blood pressure and what those numbers mean. We can look up various types of doctors and what each of their specialties entails. We can watch documentaries about doctors and the different kinds of work they do. We can call our local doctor's office and ask for a tour after hours.

Here Comes the Sun

I'm also going to let you in on a secret: we homeschool during the summer too. Please do not feel bad for my children, though. I really believe that life is a learning experience, and whether you homeschool or not, education shouldn't get a three-month break. I do not want my children to become victims of the "summer slide." It is logical to keep their brains functioning all year long instead of just August through May. Do you stop exercising for a few months a year and think your body is just going to stay in shape? That archaic school calendar was created back in the mid-1800s when much of America was rural and children couldn't be expected to be in school during the planting and harvesting seasons. They were needed at home to work. I remind my kids of this any time I ask them to mow the lawn, make their beds, or clean the house.

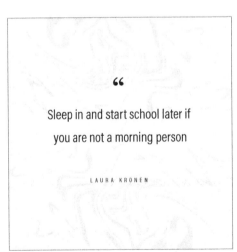

> "
>
> Sleep in and start school later if you are not a morning person
>
> LAURA KRONEN

What makes summer different from the rest of the year is

that we have less structure and no tests. It's much more laid-back, and we take advantage of the ridiculously hot Atlanta summers by swimming and going for bike rides and nature excursions early in the morning and then tackling school stuff in the afternoon when the heat is sweltering. Some days we do nothing at all school-related, but for the most part, we do have a structure to each day. I crave structure, and my kids are the same way. Author Paula White once said, "Your future is found in your daily routine. Successful people do daily what other people do occasionally."[4] It has been identified that the most successful people in the world have structure and consistency in their lives.[5] It is crucial for performance and productivity, and out of successful habits come successful people.

So, what do we do exactly during our summer homeschooling? Everyone who adds homeschooling to their summer plans will have a different approach, but both of my boys take conversational Spanish, which, unless your child plans on majoring in a foreign language or dreams of a job that requires fluency, is genuinely all you really have to know! I find public school concentrates too much on written foreign languages when many kids can't even spell in English!

My children also do standardized test prep with me all summer long, for about an hour a day. They also volunteer at various places, including an assisted-living home one day a week, and take classes in music, art, and debate outside the home. During their downtime, they are inspired to read, write, paint, and watch historical movies. We also still take our museum trips, watch plays, go on hikes, and visit historical landmarks, taking any opportunity that we can to blend learning into the day. And don't worry, they still have plenty of time to run around the backyard and play video games with their friends. However, I do believe in the proverb, "An idle mind is the devil's workshop." If you keep your child busy and a watchful eye on them, they will have a hard time finding trouble.

I think this "summer school" philosophy provides my children with virtuous values about work and learning while absolutely still letting them be kids. I long for my kids to see that that learning exists in everything we do. We never have to take a leave of absence from knowledge. I do not wish to ever portray school and learning as so dull and overwhelming that they need to take a sabbatical for three months every year. Summer is just another season, but education is lifelong!

chapter four

Homeschooling Has A Bad Rap

I never dreamt that we would become homeschoolers. I wanted my kids integrated and socialized. I yearned for their eyes to be opened to the realities of the world. I hoped and prayed for the values that we taught at home to be put to the test in the real world. From the little wisdom that I first had about homeschooling, I didn't think any of that would be possible if I kept my children at home. There is an abundance of stereotypes out there about homeschooling families, and yes, you can find some families out there that definitely nail it.

Facebook homeschooling groups are a great place to see the eclectic people who contribute to the *Saturday Night Live* parody of the "typical" homeschooler. Recently, I read a post from a mother inquiring about a formal her daughter was attending and

> "
> Talking to yourself does not make you crazy.
> It's just a parent/teacher conference.
>
> LAURA KRONEN

wondering if it was "required nowadays that she wear a slip and nylons with her dress." Nylons? Is that even a word anymore? I cannot recall a time in the last decade that I have seen a teenager wear hosiery.

Some other great questions taken from these boards:

Q *I have seven children aged eight to seventeen years old. I'm finding it hard to spend the time necessary with each one, and I feel like their education is suffering, what should I do?*

A Here's a thought: send your kids to public school. Seven kids are too many to homeschool properly. You cannot possibly give them the quality education they need with that many children and that broad of an age range at home. There are only so many hours in the day.

Q *Do you think health class can consist of watching gardening videos and reading gardening tips?*

A What? I'd probably call that "gardening class" *if* I was stretching for something.

Q *My son was seeing a therapist during his ninth-grade year, he learned a lot of coping mechanisms and had to practice them every day. Does this count as a social science elective class?*

A Hmm. I don't know? My kids eat food every day; maybe that can count as a nutrition class?

Q *Can anyone please tell me where I can get a metric conversion chart?*

A Um. How about Google?

Q *How do you explain evolution to your child?*

A See the answer above about the metric conversion chart.

These types of questions, although well intended, are the grounds for homeschoolers getting a bad reputation. Many times, when I reveal to someone that I homeschool, their facial reaction is one of utter confusion (and sometimes horror). I don't *look* or *sound* like that stereotypical homeschooler that they have heard stories of. So how could this be possible?

Ignorance is Not Bliss

There are so many clichés about homeschoolers, and I'll be honest, before I knew what homeschooling was *really* about, I was guilty of believing most of them too.

For instance, in stark contrast to the homeschooling memes, we don't wear overalls. Or, heaven forbid, denim jumpers, although my kids do sport jeans from the Gap, Old Navy, and Target. My children also change out of their pajamas

"

The things that kids will remember most about homeschooling have nothing to do with a textbook.

LAURA KRONEN

every single day. We do not sit around in sweats because a lot of our learning takes place outside of our home. Plus, picking out clothing, getting cleaned up, and dressed are essential life skills to master. That being said, in your environment, you can do what you want—because it's *your* school. That's the beauty of it!

We also don't drive a horse and buggy or sew our own clothing, and believe it or not, we have electricity *and* running water. We do not reside in a log cabin or grow our own food. Although, quite frankly, my boys would love it if we did. Hey, maybe I can count that as science class?

Another neat little freak box that homeschoolers are thrown into is that they are loners. These poor kids have no friends, and they cannot relate to other kids. I once received a message on Twitter from some ignoramus, elementary-level football coach who said he didn't want homeschooled kids on his club football team because they were *socially inept*; he also called homeschooled kids wimps. The absurdity is just mind-numbing. Nonetheless, some people believe that we are sheltered eccentrics that never leave the house.

People like to think that homeschoolers are socially awkward and lack the competencies necessary to get along with others, yet public school is so full of silent lunches, group punishments, and no talking in the hallways that the only socialization most traditionally schooled kids get is on the bus. It is a magnificent thing that my children can speak their minds to me and to each other whenever they want. Plus, they get to choose their friends because they like them and want to be friends with them, not because that person is in their class or on their team.

Every once in a while, someone likes to undermine my intelligence by professing that my kids can't quite be learning as well as if they were in public school. Can't argue there, that statement *is* true—they aren't learning *as well*; they are learning *better*.

Buckle up, because when you say that to me, I will take that opportunity to brag on my kids. My eleventh grader has taken seven AP classes with me, has fifty credits in dual enrollment at Georgia State University, and will have his associate's degree before he enters his senior year of high school. My eighth grader is on target for the same types of results. Usually letting people know those cold, hard facts quiets them down and ends with them muttering something about their patience level and not being able to have their kids at home all day. Then I feel sad for them.

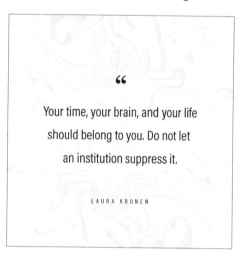

> **"**
> Your time, your brain, and your life should belong to you. Do not let an institution suppress it.
>
> LAURA KRONEN

There is also the persistent accusation that if you are your child's teacher, you can give them whatever grade you want. Generally speaking, that is true. But when it comes time for their standardized testing, the balance sheet's not going to add up. If the goal is college, you are only harming your child if you give their grades special treatment. My kids don't get all A's. They have failed tests when they don't prepare or study, but overall, they flourish. And you know why? Because they are focusing on what they love. I am making learning fun, and about them, not the masses.

A word of warning. You will have friends and family who think they know better than you. Or who passive-aggressively question you. Or who try to make you feel bad or guilty about your choice. Ignore them. Unless, of course, they are concerned about the physical welfare of your child. Then, you better listen.

Besides the misconceptions surrounding us, my children are also asked a minefield of ridiculous questions and have judgment passed on them by their peers. I used to say that there is no such thing as a stupid question, but no, *there totally is*. Here are a few:

» Are you homeschooled? How big is your farm?

» Do your parents *make you* homeschool?

» Do you hang out with friends?

» Is homeschooling even legal?

» Do you live in a compound?

» Do you actually like being homeschooled?

» Is your mom, like, your teacher?

» Aren't you sad you'll never go to the prom?

» Why would you even want to be homeschooled? It doesn't sound fun.

» When are you going back to real school?

» Do you ever leave the house?

» Quick, what's 7 times 8?

Not to be left out, I, too, am asked a slew of questions from family, friends, and strangers alike, and for entertainment purposes, I have included my usual retorts to go along with them:

Q *How can you stand being around your kids all day?*

A Um, have you not met them? My kids are fantastic!

Q *When are you going to put them in school?*

A I'm not.

Q *Don't your kids want to go to school?*

A Since they refer to it as a prison, probably not.

Q *Are you still doing that homeschool thing?*

A Are you still asking this same question?

Q *I personally think kids need school.*

A Good for you.

Q *How do you know they are keeping up?*

A We have no desire to keep up with anyone.

Q *What about socialization?*

A I have a whole chapter dedicated to answering this, but my usual response is to laugh.

Q *Better you than me.*

A Was that even an option?

Q *How do your kids make friends?*

A I don't know. How do you make friends?

Q *You must be super organized.*

A (I am, so I just agree with this one.)

Q *Do your kids get homework? How are they graded?*

A Well, since I am homeschooling, it's all "home" work, right? They have a set amount of work to get done each day, and they work until they finish. So there isn't homework per se, but there doesn't need to be. Homeschooling is completely different from traditional school. That's the beauty of it—you can make it how you want!

Q *Do they give you the stuff to teach?*

A Who are "they"?

Q *Don't you feel like sending your kids to school some days?*

A Nope. Not even once. I would never punish them like that.

Q *Are you crazy?*

A A little. The right kind of crazy, though.

Q *Do you ever leave the house?*

A Nope. Never. We have everything delivered. Our doctor even makes house calls.

Q *Do you have a teaching degree? What makes you qualified to teach?*

A I might not have a "teaching degree," but I have a bachelor's degree. Not that that even matters. It takes effort. Not a teaching certificate.

Q *Someday your child is going to have to enter the real world. Then what?*

A Are we not in the real world right now? Sitting at a desk in a brick building is less "real world" than what my kids experience every single day.

Q *You must be really smart since you homeschool.*

A Well, I'd like to think so, but the truth is, I don't know everything. Not even close. Just because I teach my kids doesn't mean I remember every detail of every subject in the sixteen years I spent in the school system. I don't think anybody does. The good news is, you don't need to!

"

Have high expectations, but make them realistic.

LAURA KRONEN

Q *How do you know what to teach them?*

A I did some research before I started as to what classes (or choices of courses) they would be taking for their grade level, and then added to it or altered it a bit. For instance, the sixth-grade curriculum in my state did not have any US history in it, and I think, as an American, my kids should learn the history of our country first. So I made an adjustment there. Elementary school and junior high school planning is a breeze once you start to focus on it. But high school gets trickier. Especially with college requirements as part of the equation.

Q *Your kids must be really well behaved.*

A We have good days and bad days—mostly good, though. And besides the rare instances of bickering during Spanish (it's the only class where they have to be sitting near each other), we are doing well! They are learning a great deal of discipline with what they need to accomplish each day, and they are also becoming self-starters, which is yet another benefit of homeschooling.

Q *Are there organized homeschool activities? Do your kids see other people? Do they play with kids their age?*

A Yes, yes, and yes. Typically I would give a more extended response, but I have an entire chapter on socialization and do not want to be repetitive.

Q *Do your kids get recess?*

A If you take "recess" to mean a break from schoolwork, I guess they get way more of it than their friends who are in a traditional school. There's breakfast and lunch breaks. (And my kids know they have it really good with the meals they have in my house! They eat so well.) Then there are fresh air breaks, have-to-run-an-errand breaks, bathroom breaks, and just let's-do-something-else-for-a-little-while breaks... It's amazing we get any schooling done.

Q *What about testing?*

A We have tests in all of our subjects. And my children participate in annual state-mandated tests. Some homeschool families are opposed to state-mandated testing, but it's really not a big deal to me. It's a good thing to see where they stand against kids in the same grade.

Q *What about high school? College?*

A I used to worry about how my children would adjust from homeschooling to going to college. But now that I see how they are learning, their keen sense of independence and their comfort level with just about anything they encounter, all of those fears have gone away.

Q *Can you homeschool someone else's kids?*

A Big NOPE! I'm putting everything I've got into my kids. You should do it for your own child. I will help you research possibilities for you to do it yourself, though.

There are edgy answers for all of these questions, but the best path to take is to avoid getting into a debate. Your family's decisions aren't up for outside scrutiny. However, if people are genuinely interested, use the opportunity to educate them. *Remember, it's one of your many proficiencies.* When people hear what my boys are doing, how knowledgeable and well-adjusted they are, and how this arrangement greatly benefits my family, it certainly makes a strong case for home education and individualized learning.

So you see, homeschooling isn't what you used to believe it to be. Forty years ago, it was just a fringe style of education. You were either a right-wing, uber-religious person or a left-wing, live-in-the-woods, wear-Birkenstocks-and-raise-goats kind of person. Over the last few decades, life has completely changed, for the good and the bad, but those derogatory ideologies are no longer the case. Homeschooled kids are actually *more* in touch with the real world and experience more real-world interaction than kids that are trapped in school all day, all learning the same exact thing in the same exact way.

chapter five

So, How Much Is This Going To Cost Me?

At the epicenter of the homeschooling experience is the curriculum, which can be brought to life, elongated and expanded, embellished, and infused with so many real-world experiences; however, the array of choices in homeschooling curricula can be overwhelming. But, likely, the idea of generating your own seems even more overwhelming.

If you're opting your child out of public or private school, it is likely because you wish to provide them with a unique type of education. So, although it's the easiest thing to do, you might not want to consider purchasing a boxed curriculum that attempts to replicate an institutional experience in your own living room. Another problem with purchasing "a grade in a box" from a one-stop-shop provider is that it is doubtful that your child is going to fit in that proverbial box. I researched this pathway thoroughly and decided it was not best option for my children. The beauty of home education should be in its tutorial method and the ability to tailor a curriculum to the particular scholastic needs of each child.

Curriculum shopping can be confusing *and* expensive, but with a little research, a little ingenuity, and using the experience of the resource you have in front of you right now (hint, hint: *this book*), you can design a curriculum for your children that makes the most of your family's strengths and resources. And once it is done, you are done for the year!

Money Can't Buy Happiness, But It Can Buy a Lot of Homeschooling Stuff

The initial step is coming up with a budget for homeschooling expenses. How much are you comfortable spending per child? If this is your first homeschooling rodeo, you are probably trying to figure it all out. Conversely, if you have been doing it for a while, you might wonder if you're spending too little or too much. Well, the fact is, if you are taking over the education for your kids, you have to be willing to spend some money to do it. Public school provides a lot of this with your tax dollars (providing you pay taxes—and for the record, I highly recommend you DO NOT commit tax evasion). So, when you think about it, you are sort of double-dipping from your own pocket to pay for homeschool. Still, the benefits of everything else that you get from homeschooling far outweigh the con of you cashing in on the money you gave Uncle Sam for your county's public school education.

Deciding on this figure will be very helpful in orchestrating a teaching plan. Little research exists to pinpoint an official average cost for homeschooling, but anecdotal evidence from national homeschooling organizations indicates costs may range from a few hundred dollars to almost $3,000 a year per student, per year depending on how frugal you are and what materials you require.[1] If you don't have a home computer or laptop and backup storage and you have to buy these materials right away, you can bet that your homeschooling budget will be more costly in your first year. I have found that I usually fall somewhere smack dab in the middle of the range. This is because I use a fusion of learning resources, and many of them are free. As a side note, I also designate money for school T-shirts each year. Every academic year we have a different color. I'm usually not corny, but sometimes we wear them on field trips to have some fun; they are always a conversation starter. You might want to think about naming your school and designing a logo or crest for shirts for your family. It is legit empowering. Our

"

Children are born optimists.
Expect the best when you embark
on a new path.

LAURA KRONEN

school is called the Kronen Academy of Arts and Sciences. We added in the *Arts and Sciences* part because those two areas are where my children shine and what we emphasize the most.

You also might want to allocate money for conventions, although I have never been to one and, frankly, do not think I would enjoy it or benefit from it because everything you could ever need is available online. Field trips and extracurricular activities are also budget line items that need to be strongly considered. The curriculum will be the bulk of where you spend your money, but think of all the money you will save on clothing or uniforms, fundraisers, and teacher presents—unless you want to purchase something pretty for yourself, which I believe, is well deserved.

My *personal* homeschooling budget breaks down to something like this per child:

- » **CURRICULUM:** Approximately $650, including online classes, resources, books.

- » **ANNUAL TESTING:** This depends on what tests they are taking. It could range from $29 for a California Achievement Test (CAT) to $300 if, for example, they were taking three AP classes and we had to pay for all three exams. You will definitely be on the lower end of the scale if you have elementary-aged children. A sensible estimation for my particular homeschooling situation is $150.

- » **SUPPLIES:** $100 for notebooks, pens, markers, pencils, sharpeners, erasers, paper, tape, glue, paper clips, folders, and art supplies. We live in a digital world, but you would be surprised by how much you still need the basics!

- » **EXTRACURRICULAR ACTIVITIES:** Approximately $500 to, well, the sky is the limit. But keep in mind you would be paying for this line item in public school as well because extracurricular activities, such as music lessons, are not free. Also homeschoolers usually try to compensate in this area a little bit more to support their children's participation with group or team activities and for specialized development of talents or skills.

» **FIELD TRIPS:** We attach great worth to deviating from the day, taking excursions and exploring the world through experience. When I factor in admissions, transportation, and additional gas money, we budget approximately $300. Maybe more. If I classify a weeklong trip as a field trip, though, I have completely blown the budget and I usually do, with no apologies.

» **MISCELLANEOUS:** Science experiments, supplies for projects, storage containers, and more than likely a slight increase in your grocery bill just because being at home all day often means more snacking. My kids chow down all day long, I have no idea where they put it all! Throw an additional $150 in for these expenses.

HOMESCHOOLING BUDGET

$150 Miscellaneous

$300 Field Trips

$650 Curriculum

$1850

$500 Extracurricular Activities

$150 Annual Testing

$100 Supplies

When I add that all up, it totals about $1,850 per child in annual homeschooling expenses. Can you do it for less? Absolutely! Can you do it for more? For sure! As a side note, adding in additional children amortizes the costs of resources, memberships, and supplies because some things can be reused or shared. Regrettably, none of the money you spend on homeschooling can be written off on your taxes, so you need to be clever and imaginative with how you keep your expenses down.

A few tips I have found to economize the yearly budget are:

» Take advantage of tax-free shopping days to purchase school supplies.

» Use your local library liberally, including the online educational subscriptions they often offer. And it goes without saying what the internet has done for homeschooling. You can find absolutely anything you need!

» Attend used book sales and homeschool curriculum fairs.

» Keep an eye out for free educational events and programs for children offered in your area. Join homeschooling groups in your area or online, and you will hear about dozens!

» Research stores and venues that offer homeschool discounts.

» Read homeschool curriculum reviews before purchasing so that you don't waste money on programs that aren't right for your student.

Every family has an individual homeschool circumstance. For example, if you've decided to homeschool your child with dyslexia because his needs were not being met at his current school, then you may need to factor in additional costs for remedial learning programs or specialized instructors. On the other hand, a family who lives in an urban setting with availability to multiple free museum programs, extensive libraries, and a robust homeschool community may be able to homeschool for only a few hundred dollars a year!

"

It will take a while to find your groove. Be patient.

LAURA KRONEN

The Right To Choose

Now, where to begin with the curriculum choices?

First and foremost, there is a big difference between online school and homeschooling. Online school is just a public school at home. It is the same horse, only in a different color. By that, I mean it is tuition-free and provides the same curriculum you would experience in your respective public school. The exception is, your child is sitting in front of a computer at home, not in a classroom. Some people might call this "homeschooling," but it really isn't. During the pandemic, this word was thrown around so much it became trite and stale. With this style of school, a parent isn't involved on any level, except making sure the kid does the work, and there is no planning involved. If your child is attending an online school, you probably do not have any need for this chapter, unless you are contemplating a new approach to his or her schooling, and I hope you are!

So, let's get back to the simplest, most no-fuss thing to do: buy a "complete curriculum," which includes the full gambit of workbooks and lesson plans for all of the subjects a child requires. There are many reputable companies out there that offer these types of curriculum packages. You can find them easily through online searches. An excellent place to source information is to join a few of the scores of Facebook homeschooling groups out there and start asking questions. Homeschool parents (mostly moms) *love* answering queries from newbies and sharing their vast knowledge and experience.

> "
> Give your child permission to make mistakes. If they have to do things perfectly, they will never take the risks necessary to discover and develop a gift.
>
> LAURA KRONEN

Really spend time researching whether or not this "complete curriculum" strategy is the avenue you want to go down. There are quite a few instances in which this one-size-fits-all curriculum may not be the best choice for your family. Cost is one obstacle for many families. A full year's curriculum can cost over $1,000 per child. Many homeschooling families are living on a single income so that the other parent can be home to teach the children. Families with multiple children incur an even greater expense. Another deterrent might be if you have a child with a learning disability, autism, or ADHD, or a gifted child that can be difficult to teach in a classroom or who excels in certain areas. Such a child may be functioning at different grade levels in various subjects, so prepackaged curricula designed for one specific grade level can be hard to use and may not produce the intended results.

These types of curricula are also set up with a thirty-six-week, five-day schedule, giving you the full 180 days of school that many states require. Having to complete the necessary work each day can make adding in extra classes, trips, and books difficult. In addition to this, a curriculum from only one source usually has the same method for teaching each level, and a child needs to be able to work with many different types of approaches and styles for future success. To decide if a packaged curriculum is the right choice for your family, you might want to ask yourself the following questions:

» Will you be working outside the home while homeschooling? If you do, you might not have the time to recreate the wheel for every subject.

» Will you be available to assist your child during the day? If you are not able to, a prepackaged choice might be the way to go.

» Have you thought about the philosophy or style of teaching you would like for your children? Does a packaged curriculum lend itself to it?

» Do you like to be hands-on? If so, a program run by someone else would not be your best choice.

» Are you highly interested in checking off lists of requirements? If so, a packaged curriculum could keep you on track.

» Do you prefer more open-ended, holistic experiences for yourself and your children? If you do, then a complete course would not work for you.

» Do you have the ability to help your child learn through the high school years? If you do, you might not need this type of educational programming.

My personal preference is to put together what my children are studying using a combination of sources. I am not a "put all of my eggs in one basket" kind of gal. However, I suggest scouting many different options before making a decision. More on other alternatives and how I design my homeschool day soon! But first and foremost, you have to decide precisely what it is your child needs to learn this upcoming year. The purpose of the next few chapters is to help guide you on this mission.

chapter six

It's Elementary

Creating your own curriculum does not require you to have a degree in education or to be an expert in every single subject. I have always felt that taking the time to put together a customized curriculum for your family can make your homeschooling experience much more meaningful *and* save you money! You just need to know your child, do your homework, and not be afraid to try things and ask for help. To initiate your homeschool adventure, the first step is to get your hands on what the public schools are requiring. You can find this through a simple online search for your county and your child's grade level. It's as easy as ABC.

The reason I begin here each year is that, firstly, I like to have a foundation to build upon. Having an idea of what is essential at each grade level is very helpful in creating a curriculum, and I do not have to recreate the wheel each year. Secondly, I want to be sure I have all of the fundamental requirements covered. My children will be taking standardized tests and AP exams in the coming months and years, and I want them to be able to excel at them.

If your state doesn't necessitate specific subject matter or standardized tests, or you do not plan on your child ever taking these tests voluntarily or ever having the slightest, little, itty-bitty chance of going back into the public school system, it is probably not necessary. Still, I have also learned it is hard to predict the future, and it is best to be prepared for any possible contingency, outcome, or scenario. Benjamin Franklin said it best when he coined this phrase of wisdom, "An ounce of prevention is worth a pound of cure."

> "
>
> No one cares as much about your child's early development as you. Trust that you know your child best and can develop your own child's strengths better than anyone else.
>
> LAURA KRONEN

To start designing your homeschool curriculum, you need to decide what it is that you want your child to learn. This is usually defined by age or grade level, and goals may be as diverse as learning the alphabet, mastering multiplication tables, gaining an appreciation for art history, or knowledge about our planet. The beauty of homeschooling is the flexibility it affords. If your children are very young, it may be enough to make structured plans for math and English and spin the other subjects around that core in a hands-on, interest-driven way. Just make a comprehensive list of everything you want your child to accomplish by the end of the school year. Many people are under the wrong impression that parents who homeschool teach every single subject, which often raises questions about qualifications for things like calculus and physics. There is no way I could teach my child calculus, although I took it myself in high school and college. Choosing to homeschool your child simply means that you've taken responsibility for the process of education and the curricular and class choices.

There are many options in every subject and at every level. As long as your child is learning, that is all that matters. And here is a newsflash: grades and test scores mean nothing until about eighth grade. However, scoring children and keeping track of grades help keep kids accountable and, generally speaking, are suitable for accounting purposes and records if you ever need to "prove" what you are doing. To be clear, I'm not talking about proving it to friends and family. You should never have to prove your decisions for your child to someone else. However, the state might question you at some point during your homeschooling life, and having records will just make your life easier. That being said, no one in my state has ever noticed or cared that my kids are not in the public school system anymore.

Outlining a general framework for introducing appropriate skills and concepts for each subject at each grade level is the way to begin. Some concepts are repeated in multiple grade levels because they act as building blocks for more complex topics. The internet will be your best friend during the planning process, but generally speaking, you can begin with this basic framework for each grade:

Kindergarten

» Learning through play is the name of the game for little ones. Give your child open-ended playthings. Toys like blocks and puppets encourage imaginative play.

» Recognizing the letters of the alphabet and the sounds of each letter, as well as practicing the writing of the alphabet fills much of the first year of school. Lowercase and uppercase letters and sight word recognition are spotlighted during kindergarten.

» Reading aloud to kindergarteners is a favorite activity for everyone involved and helps little ones make connections between written and spoken words, and acquire new vocabulary skills.

» Common science topics are insects and animals, plants, weather, soil, and rocks. It is essential to explore science-related topics through observation and investigation. Ask students questions such as "how," "why," "what if," and "what do you think."

» It is also time for children to begin understanding their role and the roles of others in the community. Police officers, firefighters, basic facts about their own country, and national holidays are all age-appropriate topics.

» Math topics include basic counting, number recognition, sorting, comparing and composing shapes, and comparing sizes of different objects.

First Grade

» Language arts consists of abstract thinking skills and reading fluency. An introduction to grammar, spelling, and writing is instituted during this year. Think of the basics: capitalization, punctuation, and simple spelling, as well as understanding compound words and definitions. Reading strategies are developed, especially focusing on the difference between reality and fiction. Elemental composition is the desired goal by the end of first grade.

» Science topics include basic economics (needs vs. wants), basic map skills, learning about the continents and different cultures.

» Math concepts include place values, addition and subtraction, telling time, measuring, recognizing and counting money, ordinal numbers (i.e., "first, second, third"), and two- and three-dimensional shapes.

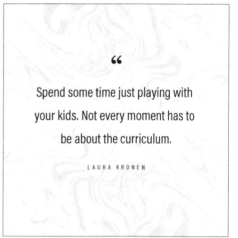

> "
> Spend some time just playing with your kids. Not every moment has to be about the curriculum.
>
> LAURA KRONEN

Second Grade

» Children of this age are usually able to understand abstract concepts. They understand sarcasm, which is good because that is my second language, and I like to use it as often as possible. They also appreciate jokes and should be starting to read at a conversational speaking rate. Use humor and silly stories to encourage creativity.

» Complex phonics concepts, vocabulary, prefixes, suffixes, rhymes, antonyms, homonyms, and synonyms should be covered. Reading fairy tales, literature, and informational text can be the primary focus of language arts lessons. You may want to introduce cursive handwriting skills at this time, although there is currently a debate about the necessity for children to learn to write in script. I personally think the only modern use of cursive is to formulate a celebrity-style signature with a little bit of flair for signing autographs and credit card charges one day.

» In language arts, identifying the sequence in a story, as well as inference and analysis, cause and effect, comparing and contrasting, and beginning use of reference tools like the dictionary are introduced.

» The scientific method is introduced in second grade, and children begin using what they know to make predictions and look for patterns in nature. Topics range from life cycles to food chains and habitats; to earth science topics like wind, water, ice, and the classification of rocks; and to force and motion concepts such as push, pull, and magnetism.

» In civics and history, advanced mapping skills and timelines are focused on, as well as topics such as Native Americans, key historical figures (such as US presidents and explorers), the United States Constitution, and the electoral process.

» Mathematically, more complex skills are introduced, odd and even numbers; adding and subtracting numbers up to 1,000; telling time from the quarter hour to the minute; fractions; measurement, data; and elementary geometry.

Third Grade

» By now, your child should know how to read, and the real excitement begins. Now, they will start reading to learn. The emphasis this year is on reading comprehension: identifying the main idea, plot, moral, and characters of the story. They will also learn to write book reports, poems, and personal narratives while learning about genres such as fairy tales, myths, general fiction, and biography.

» Grammar topics cover parts of speech, conjunctions, comparatives and superlatives, more complex capitalization and punctuation skills, and sentence types (declarative, interrogative, and exclamatory). Reading strategies become more complex. Analyzing literature, sensory devices, literary devices, and informational texts are all covered in third grade.

» Science this year focuses on living organisms, properties of matter, physical changes, light and sound, astronomy, and inherited (or genetic) traits.

» For social studies, children should be learning about different cultures and how the environment and physical land features affect the people of a given region. Other topics include the colonization of North America as well as geography topics such as latitude, longitude, map scale, and geographic terms.

» Mathematical concepts for third graders become more involved with an introduction to multiplication, division, estimation, fractions, and decimals. Arithmetic patterns and problem-solving, as well as learning about commutative and associative properties, congruent shapes, quadrilaterals, area and perimeter, time, and measurement should all be part of the course design.

Fourth Grade

» Independent work is part of a fourth-grade curriculum, and learning basic time management and planning techniques is a strong focus.

» Language arts skills for fourth graders include grammar (similes and metaphors, prepositional phrases, and run-on sentences) and composition (creative, expository, and persuasive writing). Students should also be able to compile research using sources such as the internet, books, magazines, and news reports and understand facts versus opinions, as well as points of view. Students will read genres such as folklore, poetry, and tales from a variety of cultures, and now be able to introduce descriptive details as well as organize their writing with an introduction, body, and conclusion. This is an excellent time to add a book series into the curriculum since many children at this age are captivated by them.

» Science this year focuses on the scientific process through practice. Your kitchen will now double as a science lab, as you might want your child to conduct age-appropriate experiments and document them by writing lab reports. Topics for fourth-grade science include natural disasters (such as earthquakes and volcanoes), the solar system, natural resources, electricity and electrical currents, physical and chemical changes in states of matter (freezing, melting, evaporation, and condensation), the water cycle, food chains and food webs, and how humans impact the environment. This is the year that climate change becomes an important topic for kids.

» The history of the United States, including the Revolutionary War and westward expansion, are common topics for fourth graders. There is usually a strong focus on the exploration of your home state, and it is the perfect time to take field trips exploring state parks, monuments, and other historic sites. I will always look for any excuse for a field trip; there is nothing greater than learning through experience.

» Fourth-grade students should be very comfortable with place value and adding, subtracting, multiplying, and dividing quickly and accurately. New skills to be added are factors, multiples, and patterns; equivalent fractions and adding and subtracting fractions; understanding decimals; plane figures; measuring angles; and finding the area and perimeter of shapes.

Fifth Grade

» This is the last year of elementary school and the first year that children start acting more like adults. Even though it seems light-years away, they might even know what they "want to be when they grow up." That sweet child from years prior also probably has some strong opinions by now. You might be second-guessing your homeschooling decision, but just hang in there! It's going to start getting a little more complicated, but by now, you are a pro! You can handle anything!

» Fifth-grade language arts include all of the components that are standard through the middle school and high school years: grammar, composition, literature, spelling, and vocabulary-building. Composition focuses on using proper grammar to write letters, research papers, and persuasive essays with developing and supporting arguments and sentence variety, as well as on students editing and revising their own work. The literature component includes reading books from multiple genres; analyzing plot, character, and setting; purpose and point of view.

» Popular science topics for fifth graders include the Earth and our solar system; atoms, molecules, and cells; the states of matter; the periodic table; and taxonomy and the classification system. All of these science topics lay the foundation for biology, chemistry, and physics in the high school years. At this age, children can also study health-related issues, including nutrition and personal hygiene.

» American history is a focal point of fifth grade and more detailed than ever before, studying events such as the War of 1812, the American Civil War, inventors and technological advances of the nineteenth century, and basic economics (i.e., the law of supply and demand, as well as the primary resources, industries, and products of the United States and countries around the world). This is when your child covers a lot of the trivia questions that they might be asked in a game later in life, so pay attention—it will help you too!

» Math introduces principles include decimals, operations, and dividing two- and three-digit whole numbers; multiplying and dividing fractions; mixed numbers; improper, simplified, and equivalent fractions; powers of ten; formulas for area, perimeter, and volume; graphing; converting units of measure; line plots; and properties of shapes.

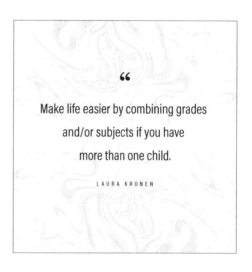

"
Make life easier by combining grades and/or subjects if you have more than one child.

LAURA KRONEN

Spark the Imagination

Regardless of grade level, do not forget to weave art, music, drama, and free play into your days. Those subjects have been slashed from some public school days in order to make time for more standardized testing, which has pressured schools to focus resources on testing subjects. Another factor for removing the arts from school is budget cuts; it's really heartbreaking to see these crucial subjects removed from the schools to create an obedient group of STEM robots. It's a wonderful thing when a student has a string of A's in their core classes. Still, it is equally beautiful when they can lead a happy, healthy, and fulfilling life and have an appreciation of art, music, and culture to enrich and expand their life experience. So even if you cannot draw a stick figure or carry a tune, teaching your child creative expression doesn't have to be hard. Visual arts, art appreciation, and art history are all exciting and under the same umbrella. You can even weave art into your study of history by learning about artists and popular schools of art during the period you are studying. If you want to find professional art instruction for your child, you can look into community classes, homeschool co-ops, online lessons (check out the Metropolitan Museum of Art's MetKids, for example), or children's events at museums and art studios. Just make sure to include creative time every day, and remember that every child is an artist and that you will want them to remain that way, with an appreciation for the arts, as they grow up.

"

Give your child unstructured time to simply daydream and wonder.

LAURA KRONEN

chapter seven

Middle School: The Worst Years Of My Life (Said No Homeschooler Ever)

There is not a solitary person on this planet that looks back on their middle school years with fondness. Unless you have been homeschooled. My now eighth-grade son insists that these junior high days have been the best three years ever! What is usually an awkward and challenging couple of years is made easier to navigate because the external stressors are removed. Students in this age group typically struggle through substantial physical and emotional changes while simultaneously enduring some of the harshest social pressures of their entire childhood. Fortunately, both of my boys seem to have skipped all that; I do not think this is due to happenstance. I fully attribute their confidence to sound parenting and homeschooling.

In creating curriculum choices for kids in middle school, it is essential to understand that they are ready for more independence. They might even want to make some of the decisions about what they're learning. It is the optimal time to start focusing on their passions and pursuing their interests and giving your tween or teen some dictum in the classes he or she takes. School is more fun when you are learning while doing the things you love.

Just like middle school, this autonomy isn't without its growing pains. Every year, you'll have to realign and fine-tune your expectations for what your kiddos can do on their own. You should expect much more detail in their written work, research, and science labs; they should also start to be more resourceful in every aspect of their life. Teach your student how to schedule their own week and be accountable. Instill worthwhile study skills within them. You shouldn't have to guide them every step of the way anymore; this is the time when homeschooling gets easier for *you*.

> "
> Learn to delegate older children to work with younger siblings in areas that you know they are proficient in.
>
> LAURA KRONEN

Another factor to throw into the mix is that your middle schoolers are dealing with changing bodies and tempestuous hormones. Little things may stress them out or cause them to become frustrated quickly, especially when they are struggling in an area and aren't quite sure how to deal with it. You don't (and shouldn't) have to fix all of their problems, but inspire them to find logical solutions. All of that being said, don't forget that your middle school students are still kids, so let them act like it. They will have plenty of time later to be adults.

The following are some suggestions for creating a sixth to eighth-grade middle school schedule:

Sixth Grade

» Math for sixth graders will include more complex concepts such as working with ratios, rates, and percentages, arithmetic operations, and properties of numbers; reading, writing, and solving variable expressions; and using the order of operations to solve problems. Remember PEMDAS (Parentheses, Exponents, Multiplication, Division, Addition, Subtraction)? Statistical thinking is introduced with data plots and frequency tables. Geometry topics are built upon, including finding the area, volume, and surface area of parallelograms, triangles, and 3-D shapes while also determining the defining aspects of circles. It's getting trickier now, isn't it? This might be the time to consider using a website or service if you have doubts about your math skills. You do not want your middle schooler to fall behind in math. It is a hard hole to climb out of.

» Science covers a lot this year, including biology: the human body and its functions; sexual and asexual reproduction; genetics; microbes, algae, and fungi; and plant reproduction. Physical science covers concepts such as sound, light, and heat; elements and compounds; electricity and its uses; electric and magnetic interaction; potential and kinetic energy; simple machines; inventions; and nuclear power. Climate and weather, space and the universe, conservation, oceans, geology, and recycling are also good topics to delve into.

» Typical social studies topics include ancient civilizations, such as the Greeks and Romans, as well as time periods including the Middle Ages and the Renaissance. Over the year, you can also focus on the US government and the Constitution, the presidential election process, and types of governments. Don't forget to add in the geography of various regions or cultures that you haven't covered before, including the history, foods, customs, and religions of each area. By sixth grade, your student should be gaining an appreciation for the fascinating and diverse world that we live in.

Seventh Grade

» Language arts is an integral part of seventh-grade course studies, as it is every year. Students will compare different versions of a work, such as a nonfiction book with its film version. They will also be expected to analyze text and infer its message, citing text to support their analysis. Your seventh grader should also be expected to produce in-depth research papers and provide well-considered and fact-supported arguments in a clear and logical format while citing multiple sources.

» Math is getting more in-depth with measurements, geography, algebra, and probability. Negative numbers, exponents, and scientific notation; prime numbers;

factoring; combining like terms; substituting values for variables; simplification of algebraic expressions; and calculating rates and proportional measurements are all topics to be broached. Geometric topics include the classification of triangles and angles, circles, and determining the slope of a line. Students should also get comfortable with graphing, interpretation, and computing basic probability.

» Science curriculum this year focuses on cells and cell structure, heredity and genetics, and human organ systems and their functions. Additional topics to be covered are the effects of weather and climate; properties and uses of water; atmosphere; air pressure; rocks, soil, and minerals; eclipses; phases of the moon; tides; and conservation and ecology. New concepts such as Newton's laws of motion; the structures of atoms and molecules; heat and energy; the chemical and physical changes of matter; elements and compounds; mixtures and solutions; and the properties of waves are all parts of a solid seventh-grade year and are building blocks for the years to come.

"

It's okay to change the curriculum midstream if it is not working for you or your child.

LAURA KRONEN

» Seventh-grade social studies has a lot of flexibility.

Usually, public schools focus the entire year on the state in which you live. For homeschooling families, you can generally cover that in a few weeks and move on to things that might be of interest to your child in the social science arena. We added mythology to ours.

Eighth Grade

» Use eighth grade as rehearsal for high school (for you and your child). It's an excellent time to begin keeping track of grades, if that wasn't something you did already, and to start keeping a transcript. Focus on weak areas, such as writing skills or speed with multiplication fact recall, so that your student is prepared for more challenging high school requirements.

» Eighth-grade language arts includes the usual: literature, composition, grammar, and vocabulary building; reading comprehension and analyzing texts; as well as being able to recognize the main idea, central theme, and supporting details of a story and to infer an author's meaning. Figurative language is a focus of this year and is always a delightful topic to teach. Composition skills should be practiced all year; eighth graders should write several essays and a variety of compositions, including how-to, persuasive, and informational articles; poetry; short stories; and research papers, with a focus on citing works and correct grammar usage.

» A typical approach of study for eighth-grade math

includes factors and multiples, algebraic and geometric concepts, measurements, and probability reading and interpreting data. Students will learn more complex numbers and operations, including scientific notation word problems. They will also focus on solving equations with one unknown variable, linear equations, and functions and systems of equations. Geometry should cover the Pythagorean theorem and geometric transformations. Data and modeling, which includes scatter plots and interpretation, will round out the year. More advanced math students might be ready to take Algebra I to obtain high school credit, while others will prepare for the ninth grade with a pre-algebra course.

"
Don't get started with schoolwork when you have somewhere to go or are in a rush.

LAURA KRONEN

» Earth, physical, and life science topics are still the areas of study in eighth grade. It seems that there is an endless amount of science to cover, and you can just keep diving deeper and deeper! My son took a physical science class in eighth grade for high school credit, and I highly recommend doing that, as they are covering most of the topics in an eighth-grade curriculum anyway. Common general science topics to cover include the scientific method and terminology, atoms, states of matter, measurement and density, elements, compounds and mixtures, ecology, conservation of mass, chemical reactions, acids and bases, the periodic table of elements; magnetism, electricity, gravitational force, light and sound waves, the motion of objects (Newton's laws of motion), and finally, simple machines. I also supplemented my children's studies with an additional engineering course in eighth grade, which they loved. As a result, I indirectly taught them some higher-level math and science concepts that have unequivocally benefited them for future years.

» Personal choices and child-led interests are usually the determining factors of a social studies course for eighth grade. Modern history, government and politics, or geography are always a safe bet. You can also add in another social science course for a second semester, like an introduction to philosophy, sociology, or world religions.

Finding Hidden Talents

Art and technology are necessities for the middle school years. This is a great time to discover new interests and talents. Perhaps your child might want to start playing a musical instrument, take up painting or drawing, create pottery, dabble in photography, join a theater club, or study art history. Technology is a huge focus in today's world. You can be sure by middle school that your child has mastered video games and every app on their cell phone, but this is also an excellent time to make sure your child is competent in using Word documents, PowerPoints, Excel spreadsheets, and knows how to conduct polls. Safety guidelines should also be stressed when using the internet; as we know, the deep, dark web can be a scary place, lurking with criminals and predators.

You can start teaching your child a foreign language as early as you like. Beginning foreign language instruction early sets the stage for fluency. Younger learners possess the capacity to develop nearly native pronunciation and intonation in a new language, and they have a natural curiosity about learning, which is evident when they engage in learning a new language. This also results in children being more open and accepting of people who speak other languages and come from different cultures.

> Keep your own passion for learning alive. Your child will be influenced by your example.
>
> LAURA KRONEN

Many states' homeschooling laws require a health course for high school graduation, so you might as well get it over with in middle school. You would think some of this is common sense by this point, considering how many PSAs our kids see on YouTube. Still, typical topics for a health course include personal hygiene, nutrition, exercise, first aid, sexual health, and the health risks and consequences associated with drugs, alcohol, and tobacco use. By the way, don't do drugs. Though I do wholeheartedly support a daily glass of wine. Or two. Not for the kids, of course. Also, whatever you do, do not omit running around, playing, and getting exercise from your homeschool day. It is necessary for a healthy body and mind!

By designing your child's curriculum, you are getting to see their imagination and world open up to new possibilities and are providing a foundation for a lifelong love of learning. It is incredible to watch as your children learn something new, master a task, or find a new interest. Don't make the mistake of being too busy planning your own homeschool curriculum or learning how to start homeschooling to enjoy the ride. The high school years come way too fast.

chapter eight

Homeschooling High Schoolers

While the primary years came naturally to me, teaching my high schooler's subjects can sometimes pose a challenge. Just because I got an A in geometry in tenth grade doesn't mean I remember how to do circle theorems or solve linear equations! On these occasions, I just get online and relearn it along with my son—if I even need to. If you have curated a self-learner during your homeschool process, you will find that they will be able to source information to learn on their own. Everything you need to know you can find on the internet, which is another steadfast reason I believe traditional school is inherently obsolete.

If you have a high school student who is college-bound, an easy way to determine which subjects they need to take is to look at the basic admissions requirements for universities and let this information drive your decision-making. Each college has its own priorities when it comes to what it looks for in applicants, so be sure to check with a range of schools that your child may be interested in to get a sense of what they should be focusing on. Generally speaking, a very solid four-year schedule would include a combination of the following:

Language Arts

Being well-read and well written is never overrated.

- » Ninth grade: More grammar, vocabulary, literature, and composition, plus public speaking, mythology, and/or poetry.

- » Tenth grade: British, American, or world literature and composition.

- » Eleventh grade: British, American, or world literature and composition.

- » Twelfth grade: British, American, or world literature and composition.

You and your child can decide what year you want to study what genre of literature. It doesn't really matter. Creative writing, speech, and debate are also outstanding thematic areas to supplement a dynamic curriculum.

Math

These math subjects are usually taken in this order:

- » Algebra 1

- » Algebra 2

- » Geometry/trigonometry

- » Pre-calculus

- » Calculus (Some colleges and/or degrees require calculus;

some don't. That is why this list includes the option of geometry/trigonometry.)

Science

These sciences are usually taken in this order:

- » Physical science

- » Biology

- » Chemistry

- » Physics

Physical science can be completed in eighth grade and another science from the elective list below can be substituted in for one of the high school years:

- » Astronomy

- » Anthropology

- » Marine biology

- » Meteorology

- » Geology

- » Botany

- » Environmental science

- » Zoology

Social Studies

These social studies courses are usually taken in this order:

» American history

» World history/geography

After world history, electives can be chosen for the remainder of the high school experience. Options may include:

» US government/civics

» Economics

» Political science

» Human communications

» Sociology

» Psychology

» Ethics

Foreign Language

Two to three years of any world language is recommended. If a foreign language is begun in seventh grade and continued through eighth grade, this will count as the equivalent of one high school year of a language. If you are fluent in another language, I do hope, for your sake, that your child chooses the language you already speak. Otherwise, you most likely will need to source out for help with this subject. *¿Comprende?*

Electives

Don't forget about these electives as well. They aid in creating progressive, robust, and compelling individuals.

- » Physical education

- » Music

- » Health

- » Art/art history

- » Digital media

- » Computer technology

Additionally, do not overlook driver's education; your child will soon be harassing you about getting his or her license. I have zero advice to give on that because I am not a supporter of all the inexperienced drivers on the road.

How to Get College Credit While in High School

Perhaps one of the most powerful features of homeschooling a high schooler is that your teen can obtain college credits while *still in high school*. There are multiple reasons your child should try to get some classes out of the way at your local college. It can make college more affordable, your child can be challenged more, and they might get through college faster! But even better than all of that, some of the classes offered on campus will take the pressure off you to teach advanced subjects like coding, macroeconomics, or environmental science, not to mention calculus or physics!

There are several ways to earn college credit while still in high school: Advanced Placement classes, College Board's College-Level Examination Program (CLEP) tests, and through dual enrollment at a local college or university.

AP and CLEP

The College Board's AP program was created in the 1950s to provide a way for super-achieving high school students to get a head start on college work. This is a massive program, consisting of thirty-eight exams, that reaches almost three million students each year.[1] In a traditional high school environment, a student would take an AP class all year long and then take the final, standardized AP exam at the end of the year and hope to get a score worthy of college transfer credit.

CLEP is also a College Board program that has been around since the 1950s. Still, it's a smaller program (currently with thirty-four different subject tests available) and is viewed as a method to demonstrate a mastery of material often taught in introductory college-level courses.[2] CLEP tests are not associated with a high school course and the schools don't promote it, so even if you attend a public school, you will need to find the curriculum for each test and learn it on your own.

> "
> When signing up for a college class, your child will usually have a choice of professors. Do not select one randomly. Use Rate My Professor (ratemyprofessor.com), which uses ratings like accessibility and humor, to get the lowdown on which professor would be the right fit for your son or daughter.
>
> LAURA KRONEN

The exam content for both AP and CLEP is developed by a panel of college professors, many of whom sit on both test development committees. Neither test is a walk in the park, but they are college courses, so they really aren't supposed to be. There are as many similarities as there are differences between the exams. Still, the most pronounced difference is their availability: AP exams are only offered in May and administered at high schools, and the CLEP is provided year-round, at multiple times in designated testing facilities so that you can take the test when you are ready. While some colleges exclusively accept AP exams (most two- and four-year colleges accept passing scores of 3, 4, or 5, depending on their academic rigor), it has become common for colleges to award credit for CLEP as well. Almost three thousand colleges and universities do![3] The passing score for a CLEP test is 50 or better, and it is probably a more straightforward test to prepare for, in my opinion.

Another big difference between AP and CLEP is that you can take an AP course in an AP-accredited school (although you *do not* have to take an official AP course to take the exam—that's why homeschooled kids can take the AP exams too!) but with the CLEP course, you are your own. There is no school that will help you with this. However, if you're homeschooled, you can creatively take the appropriate CLEP test as your final exam in the class.

What both exams have in common, though, is this: whether a teen prepares for the AP or the CLEP, they are developing the study skills and critical reasoning needed to prepare them for the transition to college. This test prep gives your student the assurance that they can successfully tackle college-level work, and the resulting college credit can give them a substantial jump-start toward completing a degree.

You can purchase study guides for AP and CLEP exams online. Of course, I have some tips and tricks to share for scoring high on any AP exam. My oldest son has taken six AP exams so far while homeschooling with me and scored 4s and 5s on all of them so that he was bestowed with the AP Scholar with Distinction award. However, when you look at the average score distributions for Advanced Placement exams on College Board's website, you will see that, on average, as many as 42 percent of the kids who take these tests DO NOT get the college credit and instead score a 1 or a 2.[4] Now, let me ask you this: if a student was in a class all year, and did all of the assignments and homework, why would they have such a good chance of failing the final exam? There is no just cause for that to happen to your homeschooled child, so after determining what AP classes your son or daughter will take, follow these simple tips.

» First, purchase the textbook that supports the information taught in this course. Always get the most recent version of the book because courses and tests change all the time, and the information that supports them can sometimes vary.

» You will also want to purchase two different AP exam review workbooks. I have looked at all of them, and the two series that I prefer are CliffsNotes and 5 Steps to a 5. (You aren't going to use the 5 Steps to a 5 books until six weeks before the test, so you can hold off purchasing them until then.)

» Now figure out how to pace your child. My son would read one or two chapters in the official course textbook at the beginning of each week. We would go straight through it without jumping around. They overlook some chapters in public school because they want to make sure they get the most "important" chapters covered first. They usually do not complete all of the information in a given year, yet all of the information is featured on the test. The College Board's official scorers seem to expect this and account for it in the grading system. But imagine if your student was exposed to *all* of the material. How much better could they do?

> "
> Homeschooling provides freedom for kids who want to try an alternate route, such as an internship or working in the family business. Don't try to force your child into a mold unsuited for them. They know themselves best.
>
> LAURA KRONEN

» Next, suggest that your student answer the questions that are at the end of each chapter as additional work. Many times, I let my son disregard the essay writing and just make sure he had mastered the multiple choice questions. The textbooks give way more information than you will ever need to know, so as long as he read it, I was pretty okay with that. It established the foundation for the next steps.

» Now comes the fun part. You are going to use a combination of resources for the next day or two of the week, and almost all of them are free. Select the Crash

Course video on YouTube (youtube.com/crashcourse) that applies to the lessons in the textbook. Also, visit Khan Academy (khanacademy.com) to reinforce the material again, if it is a STEM class.

» For the remainder of the week, enhance what your child reads with lessons on Study.com. As a side note, when you pick your courses on Study.com, be sure you are explicitly looking for classes titled with "AP classes" or "101" so that you are studying the right information. The regular "on-level" high school courses differ dramatically.

» Finally, do a review test at the end of the CliffsNotes AP review book for each chapter you finish.

» Make sure to save the full AP review tests at the end of the workbooks until the end of the year when your child will be taking practice tests. Do NOT attempt to do those during the year.

» Now let's cut to about six weeks before the test. This is when the real review starts, and we break out the 5 Steps to a 5 workbook. Each chapter is yet another comprehensive review of each area of the course. Have your child read and answer the questions at the end of each chapter. Spend a respectable amount of time focusing on weaknesses here, and when you find one, head to YouTube to watch videos to supplement each shortcoming. You can encourage your teen to find these on his or her own, but it is crucial that you follow up to make sure the work is being done. There is an abundance of superb information out there; you just need to know what you are looking for. But by this time, you are so laser-focused on AP exam prep that you will definitely recognize the gaps you need to fill.

» Lastly, two weeks before the big AP exam, have your student start the practice tests that you have been saving. Complete three or four full exams, each given three or four days apart. These should be timed and given under test-like conditions. Take note: they are long tests—about three hours each. After your child is finished, grade the test and then discuss every single question that is incorrect. Keep an emphasis on improving weaknesses, and little by little, they will start disappearing.

You may have heard that AP classes are excruciating, strenuous tests of academic fortitude. My child did not have homework on weekends or at night. We were on our own schedule and weren't paranoid if he missed a day of AP class, like the kids in public school are after the educators put the fear of God in them. Apparently, the world comes to a crashing, fiery end if even one day is missed. But keep in mind, you absolutely *cannot*, under any circumstances, just buckle down during the last six weeks and study your way to a 5 if you did not follow the rest of these steps above. That would be a surefire way NOT to get the score you want.

Whatever you do, don't forget you need to sign up to take your AP test at least six months in advance. You need to go to the College Board website (collegeboard.org) and find schools in your area that will accept homeschool students to sit the exam. Then you need to call the school and find out if they *really* will. I encountered some schools that wouldn't and some that I couldn't get a call back from. But once you locate a school that will grant your child the right to register, sign them up according to that specific school's guidelines and have them show up when the rest of the world is taking that test. It might take a little legwork, but you will figure it out. Remember, you are a homeschool parent—you are resourceful!

You need to be ambitious to take an AP exam in high school, much less a few of them a year. There is a lot of knowledge to obtain and a more sophisticated way of thinking for your child to uncover, but it is entirely doable. If you follow the steps in this chapter, your child should be extremely prepared for any AP test he or she might want to take.

Dual Enrollment

Dual enrollment programs allow academically talented high school students to take college classes while still in high school, but these college classes count as their high school classes all while obtaining college credit for the student. Sounds too good to be true, doesn't it? Some of the benefits of program participation are broadened educational opportunities, increased depth of study, and accelerated attainment of post-secondary educational goals—at usually zero cost to you. But that depends on your state and the college that you wish for your child to attend.

The first step in the dual enrollment process is to pinpoint a college near you that your child would want to attend. Most classes can be done in person or online. My son has completed both and liked both equally. However, a few on-campus professors tended to not appreciate high school kids being in their classes, and this was apparent in the way they treated him, despite his solid A performance and President's List honors. Online professors have much less face-to-face interaction (if any at all) with the students and cannot guess their age by looking at them. Dealing with the unique personalities possessed by some of those instructors was a useful life experience for my son, though, and it bothered me more than it did him.

Once you decide on a college, review the dual-enrollment section on its website. You will need to complete and submit an undergraduate application online. Many universities will require an SAT or ACT score of a certain level to gain

> **"**
>
> Don't change the way you are homeschooling when your child enters high school —stick with what works!
>
> LAURA KRONEN

admission into the program. However, numerous community colleges do not require standardized test results. You will also need to submit your student's official high school transcripts. If they were educated at a non-accredited homeschool or through a homeschool program that hasn't been approved by the college, they're considered a homeschool applicant.

You will also need to submit identifying documents, such as a driver's license or passport. Remember, there are deadlines for the admissions process, so you will want to check those out and act in a timely fashion. Once admitted, you will want to transfer any AP or CLEP credits that your student has earned in their prior high school years to start carving out their pathway to a degree.

Every state has different rules and regulations when it comes to dual enrollment, and they change regularly. My junior in high school will be receiving his associate's degree, with a total of sixty credits, from Georgia State University before he even graduates high school. This is an impressive feat and shows how heavy his course load was and how intensely he has been working. However, the state of Georgia has caught on to this and does not want to be paying for a free college degree for high school students. As such, it has now mandated that the maximum number of credits a new dual-enrollment student can earn is thirty. Luckily my son enrolled before then and will even be able to take part in GSU's graduation ceremony! Sadly, my younger son will not have the same good fortune, but we will find other ways to make an impression in our personal homeschool world.

There is a lot of confusion around dual-enrollment requirements. You will probably hear the word "hold" a lot. There is always a hold on your child's account for something, whether it be the need for updated emergency contact information, state funding, financial aid, or participation agreement forms. You will not be able to register for classes without removing these holds. Your best bet is to call the dual-enrollment office at your college or, better yet, stop in there to get it all figured out.

Registering for classes is only done during certain weeks for dual-enrolled students. You must pay strict attention to these dates. If you miss deadlines, not only will your child have the worst choice of professors, but he or she might not be able to register at all.

You might be wondering what classes your student should take for dual enrollment. They should fulfill all of their high school level courses first. Of course, taking them at a college will be harder than it would be if they were just taking the course at home since it is for college credit. Your child might also have to take College Board's ACCUPLACER tests (accuplacer. collegeboard.org) to see what level they will need to be placed at for certain courses, including math and foreign languages. Keep in mind, early college courses aren't for everyone. Every child is different, and by working together you can figure out the best path for them.

chapter nine

Co-Ops And Curricula

You now have an overall idea of what each year of homeschooling resembles for your child, so where do you find the resources to design each 180-day period? You might want to begin by making use of your local community. There are likely to be homeschool co-ops in your area and people offering classes in a variety of topics. A homeschool co-op is an assembly of families who come together and work cooperatively to achieve common goals. Co-ops can be organized around academics, social time, the arts, activities, crafts, service work, or projects—or some combination of these.

Co-ops can be parent-led, or the parents may chip in to pay all or some of the teachers and activity leaders. They can be as large as a few hundred children or as small as two likeminded families, and may meet in many different places, including homes, churches, libraries, and community centers. There are no hard and fast rules, but a co-op's meeting frequency and yearly calendar is up to the co-op organizers. Meetings might range from once a week or twice monthly to once a month. Occasionally co-ops model themselves after universities (albeit the co-ops are unaccredited) and meet once, twice, or three days a week with a full docket of homework to completely cover typical academic credits. Still, most of the work is completed at home. Other co-ops are more creatively focused, with arts, social time, and occasionally a different spin on traditional topics. Children in these co-ops typically do most of their knowledge-based learning outside of the co-op, while the co-op is a chance for them to socialize, get out of the house, and do something different.

Personally, I did not join a co-op. I started homeschooling because I wanted a hands-on approach (*my* hands, specifically)

> Once upon a time, all children were homeschooled.
>
> LAURA KRONEN

with my kids and did not want others teaching my children. My children are also involved in a variety of extracurriculars, so we didn't feel the need for more socialization. The co-op path wasn't the right choice for us, but a significant number of families find it to be valuable support.

I constructed my children's programs through a combination of resources. One of the things I did not approve of when my children were in public school was the Common Core method of teaching, so we do everything in our power *not* to adhere to that. In fact, in an extreme act of nonconformity, I taught my kids to carry the one.

Common Core was launched in 2009 to "ensure all students, regardless of where they live, are graduating high school prepared for college, career, and life."[1] What it really is, is a failed educational approach that undermines and limits parental choice and shuts their voices out of their children's education and that leaves little to no room for teachers to innovate and meet the unique needs of their students. This one-size-fits-all government-driven educational policy assumes that every student learns precisely the same way. Funny thing is that it actually does what it set out not to do: leave no child behind. Some states are waking up to this, like Florida, for example. The *Miami Herald* recently reported that Governor Ron DeSantis announced the creation of new academic standards to root out all "vestiges of Common Core" and change the way Florida's students learn, with DeSantis stating, "It goes beyond Common Core to embrace common sense."[2]

Many other states are still far away from phasing out Common Core, and no one was even thinking about eradicating it back when I started homeschooling. Although I look to the school districts to begin my yearly planning, this is merely to establish an outline, not for their curriculum to serve as my homeschool bible. I assembled my full curricula using a team of resources.

66

Allow your family's
needs to shape your schedule.

LAURA KRONEN

I have no desire to make this book an advertisement for any individual company. Still, there are many brilliant educational tools that have contributed to making my children's education a cut above the rest, and they need to be given props. Note that none of these companies have given me a free product or any compensation for inclusion.

Keep Your Options Open

STUDY.COM

This has been, hands down, my greatest asset. Study.com has everything you could ever want and more, and is the largest, most extensive website for education seekers. This subscription-based resource has over 27,000 video lessons on almost any subject you can think of, starting with middle school and going up to the college level. This company has been in existence since 2002 and services tens of millions of students each month. Its platform is super easy to use, and the quality of the content is stellar. This is always a go-to for me when planning my children's courses. You can even get college credit for many of the courses, all of which are transferable to over 2,000 different universities.[3] There are different levels of subscription service to Study.com; I have always used the premium edition. The basic edition does not offer any of the benefits—mainly quizzes, tests, and tools for tracking progress—that I utilize for my boys.

KHAN ACADEMY (KHANACADEMY.COM)

I do not know what I would do without Khan Academy when it comes time to anything related to core subjects. This absolutely, 100-percent free resource offers practice exercises, instructional videos, and a personalized learning dashboard that empower learners to study at their own pace and that makes it really easy for parents to keep track of it all. Math, science, engineering, computer programming, economics, history, art history, economics, and more are all available here. They boast state-of-the-art, adaptive technology that identifies strengths and learning gaps. Additionally, they have partnered with institutions like NASA, the Museum of Modern Art, the California Academy of Sciences, and MIT to offer specialized content. They even have Advanced Placement, SAT, LSAT, and MCAT test prep programs. Did I mention this was all free? Every once in a while, they ask for a donation, which you will feel more than happy to give when you behold all the benefits you get from Khan.

IXL (IXL.COM)

IXL is available as a monthly or yearly subscription and offers educational resources in math, language arts, science, social studies, and languages. It is meant for children in kindergarten and up, but I feel that by tenth grade, your child will have outgrown this platform. This is an excellent resource for elementary and middle school students to practice skills and to

> "
> Homeschool your children not to prepare them for tests, but to prepare them for life.
>
> LAURA KRONEN

earn awards for them. Everyone loves a fun surprise and acknowledgment of working hard. What I love about IXL is that it tells the student why they got the problem wrong. It tracks which problems your child is struggling with and will not allow them to complete the skill until mastered, and you can view the analytics for your child as they go along. IXL is bright, current, colorful, and fun.

YOUTUBE

Where do you go when you need information on absolutely anything at all? YouTube! The amount of quality (and crazy) information you can find on YouTube is almost overwhelming. There is an endless amount of instructional content found here. Anytime I want to supplement a lesson (which is almost always), I turn to my favorite channels: Crash Course, TedEd, Geography Now, Real Engineering, ASAP Science, Bozeman Science, History, Amoeba Sisters, and the list goes on! Start with these, but I am sure you will find your favorites as well. Make sure you put your YouTube parental filters on if you are letting your child have free rein on YouTube; inappropriate content is just a click away!

MEL SCIENCE (MELSCIENCE.COM)

Learning scientific principles is essential even if you don't plan to become a scientist. The best way to learn science is to combine theory with a hands-on approach, and performing experiments with your children is a learning experience and quality time blended together. Plus, practical experiments are a great way to inspire curiosity and to engage kids to encourage a greater interest in science. I enrolled in the MEL Science subscription box service for a year, and it was money well spent.

Safe and engaging science experiments are delivered to your door monthly and can be used to supplement lessons or as add-ons to any science curriculum. I think they are appropriate for kids from middle school to tenth grade. Although they might be a little easy for a tenth grader, the chemistry behind the experiments can be very complex and can be explored on a deeper level. And what kid doesn't love chemical reactions and attempting to blow stuff up?

NEWSELA (NEWSELA.COM)

Newsela is a mostly free, up-to-date content provider of an expansive library of engaging real-world content that is timely and relevant and can supplement your instruction in almost any subject and is appropriate for all ages. News stories come from respected sources such as *Scientific American, The Guardian,* the Associated Press (AP), *USA Today, The Economist,* and the History Channel, among many others.

TEACHERS PAY TEACHERS (TEACHERSPAYTEACHERS.COM)

Teachers Pay Teachers is a fantastic place to turn to when you are looking for lesson plans that you do not want to create yourself or to supplement your own lessons. Look here for pre-K through grade twelve resources, knowledge, and inspiration to teach at your very best. They offer more than three million free and paid resources created by educators who understand how hard it is to always be creative. Often I find PowerPoints, worksheets, quizzes, and tests on specific material that would require too much work for me to make myself. This is fantastic if I've been too busy with work or, frankly, I just didn't feel like doing it. Helpful hint: always purchase products with answer keys, unless you want to spend your time figuring out all of the answers out yourself. I think you probably have better things to do.

826 DIGITAL (826DIGITAL.COM)

This is a treasure chest of highly engaging and ready-to-use topic- and genre-based writing materials for budding writers from grades one to twelve. The website is free to use with sign up, although donations are encouraged. Many times it is hard to come up with yet another writing assignment; this resource will solve all of those problems. So, whether you want to focus on specific skills, inspire creativity, or produce a polished piece with your student, this is the place to go.

Full Educational Programs

Occasionally I look to outsource some subjects because I do not have the time or the advanced knowledge to teach effectively, or I just want someone to push my child harder than I would in certain areas. For each child, this experience has been in a different subject. This past year it was language arts for my eighth grader and physics for my junior in high school. I have listed below a few unique programs that are worth checking out, but please do your research as to what looks like the best fit for your child because there are dozens out there.

EXCELSIOR CLASSES (EXCELSIORCLASSES.COM)

The word "excelsior" is a Latin word that means "always upward" and indicates a desire to continually improve. Excelsior Classes is an educational platform with a commitment to continuously propel students higher with live classes and stimulating instruction by passionate subject matter experts. Opportunities for interactive dialogue with instructors and other students abound. I find that the teachers really care about the students and are incredibly knowledgeable in their subject area. All courses

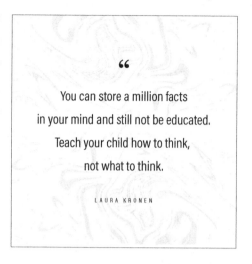

> **"**
> You can store a million facts in your mind and still not be educated. Teach your child how to think, not what to think.
>
> LAURA KRONEN

are couched within a Christian worldview, and although that wasn't my intention in choosing Excelsior, I found that for some classes it was an added benefit to have a class with a Christian viewpoint. There's nothing wrong with a little more God in our daily lives.

THINKWELL (THINKWELL.COM)

Thinkwell creates dynamic, video-based learning materials for core curriculum subject areas. Thinkwell's online video courses feature engaging lessons from award-winning professors, along with automatically graded exercises and more. It's like having a world-class university professor right by your side. I am currently using this platform as a supplement for my son's AP Biology class.

DEREK OWENS (DEREKOWENS.COM)

Although the instructor is a little quirky and dry, my son absolutely loved learning physics with Derek Owens. This professor offers a few different science classes and assigns a lot of work, but you will appreciate not having to create the high-level programs yourself—or struggle to relearn it for that matter.

HOMESCHOOL SPANISH ACADEMY (SPANISH.ACADEMY)

Hola! Homeschool Spanish Academy offers Spanish curricula for all ages, from preschool to adult. You can schedule classes for any day of the week and can take them on your own or share classes with others and save money. The website and learning platform are straightforward to use, and scheduling live online classes on the date and time you prefer with your desired teacher is pretty simple. The value that you are getting and seeing how fast your child is learning are worth the price of classes.

EASY PEASY ALL-IN-ONE HOMESCHOOL (ALLINONEHOMESCHOOL.COM)

This free online resource was created by homeschooling parents for homeschooling parents. It contains a full homeschool curriculum from a Christian perspective for grades K-12. It's all planned out day by day, so children can go to their level, scroll down to the lesson they are on, and follow the directions. Easy peasy, lemon squeezy!

CODE.ORG (CODE.ORG)

Code.org is a fantastic organization that offers a structured computer science curriculum for the littlest of computer programmers to AP level students. Lessons teach the many different types of coding with captivating videos and games. Kids pace themselves, and most work is done independently, which was good news to me because computer coding is just not my thing.

MASTERCLASS (MASTERCLASS.COM)

I cannot express to you how much I love this extensive collection of courses from some of the world's best minds. You will find thousands of classes from inspiring individuals in the music and entertainment industry, culinary arts, design, photography, fashion, sports, science, business, politics and society. Names like Neil deGrasse Tyson, James Patterson, Samuel L. Jackson, Natalie Portman, Usher, Penn & Teller, Chris Voss, Anna Wintour, Wolfgang Puck, Annie Leibovitz, Bobbi Brown and dozens more share their stories, skills, shortcuts, failures and successes. These classes are geared towards middle school through adult, and you will find your student (and yourself) fascinated and looking forward to each new episode.

A Few More to Think About

Below I have listed a couple of more resources that I have researched but not *personally* used yet, but have heard other homeschool parents have great success with. While you are discovering the alternatives, remember to keep in mind how the content, the approach and the delivery will work for the individual needs of your child. Many parents, like myself, find that combining different curriculums is sometimes the best approach; others feel very comfortable with going with just one company. My way is not the *only* way, so feel free to explore these other options when evaluating the needs of your family.

- » 7 Sisters Homeschool (7sistershomeschool.com)

- » Abeka (abeka.com)

- » Acellus (acellus.com)

- » Apologia (apolgia.com)

- » Art of Problem Solving (artofproblemsolving.com)

- » Brave Writer (bravewriter.com)

- » Calvert Homeschool (calverthomeschool.com)

- » GeoMatters (geomatters.com)

- » Global Student Network (globalstudentnetwork.com)

- » MasterBooks (masterbooks.com)

- » Math U See (mathusee.com)

- » Mr. D Math (mrdmath.com)

- » Outschool (outschool.com)

- » Power Homeschool (powerhomeschool.com)

- » Sophia (sophia.org)

- » Teaching Textbooks (teachingtextbooks.com)

- » Timberdoodle (timberdoodle.com)

- » Wild World of History (wildworldofhistory.com)

chapter ten

Standardized Testing

Standardized testing is the best way to fairly and accurately assess a student's capability...said no one ever.

Standardized testing might even be a hotter topic than vaccinations for parents who have elected to take their children out of public school and educate them at home. Those who end up on the "con" side of the argument and choose not to do standardized testing at all might cite some of the following negative attributes of standardized testing:

» Standardized testing does not consider the fact that many children are just not good test takers or that a child might be having a bad day on the day of the test.

» Many teachers "teach to the test." This can decrease a student's learning potential based on the material that the class focuses on. If something is fascinating, riveting, or beneficial to the development of a student's comprehension of the world, but it will not be on the standardized test, then there isn't any incentive for the teacher to cover this material. Instruction time is being exhausted by insipid test prep.

» Because students know that test scores may end up affecting their futures, they do whatever it takes to pass them, including cheating and taking performance-enhancing drugs.[1]

» Standardized tests do not value creativity. Ever. It's a black-and-white Scantron world.

» Standardized tests are a vague assessment of teacher performance, yet they are used to reward and punish teachers. Their students' scores may affect their salaries and job security. (Check out the best seller, and one of my favorite books, *Freakonomics* by Malcolm Gladwell for some interesting statistics on this).[2]

» Standardized testing does not evaluate the growth of a student over a full academic year, but rather at a snapshot in time.

» Standardized tests do not value diversity, and yet students who take standardized tests have a magnitude of different life experiences: they come from different cultural backgrounds, have various levels of proficiency in the English language, unique learning and thinking styles, and diverse families. And yet the standardized test treats them as if they were all precisely the same, identical to the group that took the test many years ago, which the test used to establish its norm or standard for grading comparison.[3]

» Standardized tests favor those who have socioeconomic

blessings. Multibillion-dollar test companies not only generate the tests, but they also manufacture the prep courses and programs offered to help students do well. If you have the dough, you can even hire specialized tutors. However, if you don't have the cash or your school is in a lower socioeconomic district that gets less funding than wealthy suburban schools, then you're not getting the same test prep as those at higher socioeconomic levels. It seems pretty shady, doesn't it?

» Standardized tests occur in a learning environment that is artificial. They're timed, you can't talk to or ask questions of anyone around you or use any reference tools. You can't even get up and go to the bathroom unless it's a designated

> "
> College is NOT the only path your child can take after high school. Standardized tests might not be something you even have to worry about!
>
> LAURA KRONEN

bathroom break. This sounds like imprisonment to me, not a bona fide real-world scenario. When children are being watched and timed, they naturally feel more worried and tense.[4]

» Standardized tests create even more stress. Some kids do well with stress. Other students crumple from test-day nerves. So, again, this is an example where not everyone has an equal and fair chance of succeeding. The

Sacramento Bee once reported that "test-related jitters, especially among young students, are so common that the Stanford-9 exam comes with instructions on what to do with a test booklet in case a student vomits on it."[5] Gross. But true.

» Standardized tests reduce the entire human experience of learning to multiple-choice questions. A student may have a vast knowledge of a topic but receive no recognition for it because of a low test score. If the student were able to paint a picture, give a speech, or create a hands-on project, they could showcase that knowledge. No such luck at a proctored testing facility with no way to demonstrate it.

» Standardized tests weren't developed by the great scholars or geniuses of the world. They were developed by didactic minds with bookish educations. To my knowledge, Albert Einstein never created a standardized test (although he failed a whole bunch of them). Einstein knew what he was talking about when he said, "A true sign of intelligence is not in knowledge, but in imagination." Einstein was homeschooled, by the way.

» Open-ended questions on standardized tests are often graded by temporary workers with no specific educational training on the subject being graded. And, no, you do not get to debate your score.

» Standardized tests give parents and teachers a false sense of security. You might think that if a student scores well on a test, then they know the material, but the student may have simply memorized the fact or formula or trick necessary to do well on the test. In Howard Gardner's book *The Disciplined Mind: Beyond Facts and Standardized Tests, the K-12 Education that Every Child Deserves*, it was reported that a group of Harvard graduates were asked why it is colder in the winter and warmer in the summer. Believe it or not, most of them got the question wrong. They were obedient, bubble-filling test-takers but didn't understand fundamental principles that required a more profound comprehension.[6]

» Standardized testing pigeonholes students as "winners" and "losers." The winners are trapped, caught up on a hamster wheel of achievement that they must stay on at all costs. They do not want to let anyone down, and they will go on to further their education. After all, they are the smart ones. Inversely, the losers suffer a loss of self-esteem, self-confidence, and the damage of low future expectations.

» Standardized testing has not had a measurable impact on student achievement over the years. (At least I can't find any data supporting that it has.)

Standardized testing sounds absolutely abominable, doesn't it? But it does have its benefits. I am not a huge fan, but I am a semi-supportive proponent of it for my children, mainly because I don't want to make it difficult for them to get into college. We know that standardized test scores are weighed particularly heavily in the evaluation of homeschooled students' college applications.[7] Because colleges do not know much about the design of an individual student's homeschooled courses, and since homeschooled students are given such flexibility in course selection, colleges depend strongly on the additional chance to assess the student's academic ability in a standardized setting.

"

Your child is way more than just a test score.

LAURA KRONEN

Another personal reason I have for my children to take standardized testing is that it is validating for me to see how they compare to their peers in a traditional school, a little proof of progress for all of us. I do not need confirmation of my homeschooling methods, but it is a good feeling to know you are setting your children up for success. I never ever "teach to the test," though. In fact, it's quite the opposite. My children took the Iowa and the CAT tests in elementary school and middle school, and then AP Exams, the PSAT, the SAT, and the ACT in high school. An excellent source to purchase standardized tests is Seton Testing (setontesting. com). In addition to the Iowa and CAT tests, they also offer the Terranova and Stanford 10 and have a simple comparison chart to detail out the differences between all of them. We never prep for any of the elementary or middle school tests, and the only preparation we do for any standardized test is a workbook I purchase on Amazon a few weeks before the exam.

Arguments in favor of standardized testing might be:

» Standardized testing aids teachers in determining precisely what to teach and when to teach it. This saves instructional time and provides a clear and concise method for the distribution of information.

» Standardized tests are dependable and impartial measures of student achievement. Multiple-choice tests in particular are graded by machines and therefore are not victims of human subjectivity. Additionally, if they were not implemented, policymakers would have to be dependent on tests scored by each student's school and its idiosyncratic teachers. The latter has a biased and vested interest in producing "favorable" results.

» Like I previously mentioned, one of my reasons for supporting standardized testing is that it provides parents with the data that allows them to determine how their child is doing in comparison to other students, both locally and nationally.

» Ninety-three percent of studies on student testing, including the use of large-scale and high-stakes standardized tests, found a "positive effect" on student achievement, according to a peer-reviewed, hundred-year analysis of testing research completed in 2011 by testing scholar Richard P. Phelps and reported in his book, *Defending Standardized Testing*.[8]

» "Teaching to the test" can be a smart way of educating because it focuses on the essential information and skills needed to prepare students for future studies while eliminating activities that don't produce knowledge gains.

» Most students and parents feel that standardized testing is fair, according to a Public Agenda survey.[9] Most teachers and administrators agree and acknowledge the importance of standardized tests and do not feel their teaching has been compromised. Standardized tests provide a lot of useful information at a low cost, and consume little class time. A poll conducted by the Associated Press–NORC Center for Public Affairs Research in June and July 2013 found that 75 percent of parents say standardized tests "are a solid measure of their children's abilities," and 69 percent say the tests "are a good measure of the schools' quality." Ninety-three percent of parents say standardized tests "should be used to identify areas where students need extra help" and 61 percent say their children "take an appropriate number of standardized tests."[10]

» The multiple-choice format used on standardized tests generates precise information that is necessary to assess and improve schools. Today's multiple-choice tests are more sophisticated than their predecessors. The Center for Public Education, a national public school advocacy group, says many "multiple-choice tests now require considerable thought, even notes, and calculations, before choosing a bubble."[11]

» Many professions require standardized tests to be able to practice their craft. Physicians, lawyers, real estate brokers, and pilots all have to take high-stakes standardized tests to ensure they have the necessary knowledge to perform at the highest standards.

The cold, hard fact reported by the *Washington Times* is that homeschooled students tend to perform *above* the national average on the SATs (in fact, 72 points higher) and the ACTs (the average score is 21 and homeschoolers test out at 22.8 out of 36 points). Homeschoolers also perform at the seventy-seventh percentile on the Iowa Test of Basic Skills. The paper also has pointed out that, "There are two main factors

> "
> Standardized tests can't measure passion, strength, compassion, common sense, empathy, personality, grit, life skills, creativity, intuition, morals, motivation, or a love of learning.
>
> LAURA KRONEN

for these outstanding results: the educational environment where learning takes place and the individualized, one-on-one instruction. Most homeschool students are directly taught by their parents, who love their children enough to make the sacrifice to make sure their child is taught in a safe and loving learning environment. Second, one-on-one instruction emphasizes the best interests of the child rather than the best interests of the group."[12]

According to the National Center for Education Statistics (NCES), homeschoolers tend toward higher academic achievement for a variety of reasons. Homeschoolers generally come from homes that include educated parents with higher-than-average incomes, and higher-income parents tend to be less inclined toward divorce. Also, homeschooled kids on average watch less television than do students educated in public schools.[13]

Furthermore, you should check your state's requirements because at least twenty states *require* standardized testing for homeschool students.[14] Furthermore, college attendance often hinges on SAT or ACT scores, and in many cases, not taking these tests at all will make it much harder to get into college than it would be just to take the tests and not do well. Standardized tests, while not ideal, are sometimes mandatory, and the best thing a parent can do is prepare their student for at least some standardized testing, set them up for a favorable outcome, and rest assured that homeschooled students tend to do better on standardized tests than their public school counterparts.

If your homeschooled student is hoping to attend a top university, you should pay close attention when it comes to preparing for standardized tests. Comparison to similar students is one of the only ways admissions committees can measure the significance of an individual student's accomplishments, which makes evaluating homeschooled students particularly challenging. Regardless of the rigor of a student's course load, colleges cannot determine academic achievement using grades alone.

Whatever your take on standardized testing is, and whether your state requires it or not, you have an abundance of resources available for you to decide what is right for your child. Proof of progress can be a very reassuring validation to all of your tremendous efforts.

Can A Homeschooled Kid Get Into College?

We have established that standardized testing is a requirement for most college admissions. However, most of the information in the college admissions arena is geared toward students who attend a traditional high school. You can find information about which classes to add to your schedule, what types of teachers to get letters of recommendation from, and learn how colleges will compare you to students who also attend your high school. But what about us homeschoolers?

For many homeschooled students and their parents, the world of college admissions can be confusing and foreign, and you need to filter through a lot of information. And, of course, standardized testing isn't *all* that is considered for college admissions. Grades and extracurricular activities play a big part. A great platform for free college guidance is College Vine (collegevine.com), which offers a plethora of information geared toward the college admission process that can be extremely helpful to homeschoolers. I'm currently using it to weigh my older son's potential for admission to his top three schools.

Standing Out in a Crowd of One

A homeschool education can be just as dynamic as any traditional school's. However, a major difference is that while conventional schools standardize across the board, homeschoolers are bound by few restrictions. A homeschool education caters to particular needs and strengths instead of primary state or college requirements. Course options are endless instead of dictated by the district. Students are free to design a school schedule that allows flexibility for travel, work, or extracurricular commitments. This luxury is not often afforded to most traditionally educated students.

Homeschoolers can present some complexities for admissions committees, though. There is such diversity among high schools in terms of academic rigor, extracurricular offerings, and socioeconomic status that colleges, rightfully so, tend to compare applicants to students from their school or from a similar area in order to understand their achievements in the context of the opportunities available to you. You just can't do that with homeschooled students.

> "
> Download a handy app called CollegeHunch, which will give you quick and concise information on colleges and universities at your fingertips.
>
> LAURA KRONEN

Because homeschooled students typically do not have classmates, aside from their siblings, it can be challenging to gauge how an A in a homeschool course stacks up to an A in a traditional course, unless the class is an AP class with an accompanying standardized test. For this reason, taking the homeschool equivalent of an AP course and showing up for the end-of-the-year test is a good idea for students looking to show off their academic chops to admissions committees. Remember, earning the title of valedictorian of your homeschool consisting of a party of one is remarkably different from being the valedictorian in a graduating class of five hundred.

To stand out, it helps to take those AP classes, or to become dual-enrolled at a local college, especially if you have no other standardized test scores. Final grades in demanding courses such as these can give colleges a point of reference regarding a homeschooled student's capabilities. They also demonstrate drive and a willingness to challenge oneself, something colleges look for primarily in homeschooled applicants.

A Little Extra

Admissions committees consider the extracurricular accomplishments of homeschooled teens in a different light. A homeschooled high schooler has full discretion over the amount of time they spend on academics, and has the freedom to work at their own pace. The typical traditionally schooled student spends eight hours a day in school regardless of how long it actually takes them to absorb the material. Colleges will want to see what your homeschooled child did with this "extra" time. You'll want to have something to show for it. Academic teams, service projects, volunteering, and starting a small business are all application-worthy and can set your child apart from other applicants.

Colleges seek creative, self-determined go-getter behavior much more in the homeschooled applicant than in the traditional applicant. Admissions officers want to ensure that applicants have taken full advantage of the freedom homeschool has provided. Hence, students who can demonstrate strong themes of leadership and ingenuity have a decent shot at admissions to the nation's most competitive schools. So, set the bar high!

If You Didn't Write it Down, It Never Happened

Another part of the college application process is the submitting of a transcript. This is the reason you have been keeping such accurate records (I hope!) because it is your obligation to create a high school transcript and send it to prospective colleges. You can create it yourself; you can generate it from a homeschool tracking program; you can enlist a service that does it for you; or you can even join a homeschool group that produces professional transcripts as part of your dues.

Because the day-to-day of homeschooling often looks quite different from a traditional setting, trying to turn a student's academic experiences into courses and credits may seem like a daunting task. However, parents can rest assured knowing there is no such thing as a "correct" or "standard" transcript even among school districts. I cannot stress enough though that, to keep it from being an insurmountable task at the end, you should keep meticulous records of courses, course descriptions, and grades.

Your transcript should include all of the following information:

» The student's name, the name of your homeschool (if applicable), address, and phone number.

» Your student's high school course list ordered by year (grades 9-12). Those earlier years don't matter unless your child took a high school test in eighth grade.

» The location where each class was taken (i.e., at home, an online institution, community college, or university).

» The grading scale being used in your homeschool.

» Your student's overall GPA.

» Credits given per course (listed per semester and per year).

» Expected graduation date.

» Parent signature with a date.

If you've taken classes online or outside of your homeschool, contact each organization to make sure they send the official copy of your transcript to prospective colleges. These institutions will not just take your word for it. The transcript you create should be cumulative and include both homeschooled classes and any classes taken at an outside establishment.

Another way to go about creating a transcript and making things easier for yourself is to collaborate under an accredited "umbrella school" that produces official transcripts and diplomas and that will not only take care of those tasks but will also help with many other official functions. However, there will be a price to pay, both monetarily and in giving up a wee bit of control.

Nice But Not Necessary

Educational accreditation is a quality assurance process that evaluates educational institutions, policies, practices, programs and learning conditions and determines if recognized standards are met. The US accreditation process was developed in the late 19th century saw the need to coordinate a level of requirements with secondary and post-secondary institutions.

Accreditation doesn't mean the school you might partner with is superior to one that isn't accredited; however, they could dictate a particular approach or method for your family's homeschooling requirements. I have found that many such schools are relatively lax and let you do your thing as long as you meet specific criteria. The best outcome that arises from accreditation is peace of mind knowing that your *t*'s will be crossed and your *i*'s dotted. If you find the right accredited school, you can have free rein over what you are doing as long as you run it by the powers-that-be.

> "
> You've taught your homeschooler to be independent and self-motivated.
> I'd say they're more ready for college than most kids their age!
>
> LAURA KRONEN

There are other significant reasons to look into aligning yourself with an accredited institution. If there is the slightest chance that your child might return to public high school one day, then transferring credits becomes a serious matter. It's a whole lot easier to do this with accredited school credit on your high schooler's transcript. If your high schooler intends to pursue sports in college, more in-depth records are necessary, so some may find it easier to use an online or virtual school and be evaluated as part of a nontraditional program rather than a true homeschool program.

If you find the right accredited school, they will also handle all of your dual-enrollment funding and push paperwork when needed. What's more, they most likely have an affiliation with organizations such as the National Honor Society, which might be relevant to you and your student. Also, word to the wise, don't be fooled by the sham "honor societies" who try to make you pay to join. You might as well print up a certificate that says your child was in the "Homeschool Honor Society." It carries about the same weight.

But before racing down the credentialed road, keep in mind that no state *requires* that a homeschool program, curriculum, or diploma be accredited.[1] That's fortunate for all of us because you have less than a zero percent chance (if that's even possible) of being able to apply for accreditation for your homeschool. Thankfully, most institutions of higher learning do not require this either, although, as with anything, there may be a few exceptions.

Remember, while accreditation does not *guarantee* academic quality, it does ensure that there is oversight and adherence to standards. If you *do* choose to affiliate with a traditional school for your college-bound student's benefit, you might as well look for one that is accredited.

That Magic Piece of Paper

Homeschoolers do not need a GED or a diploma to apply to college or to qualify for financial aid; instead they just have to declare that their homeschool education meets state law requirements. And I'm positive by now that you looked up your state's requirements, right? Most choose not to take the GED if they have valid transcripts, which I have already stressed the importance of ad nauseum, as colleges will place the greatest emphasis on your transcript and standardized test scores. If you do not have either of those things, the GED might be the way to go. If your student is homeschooled through an online or virtual school, an affiliate school, or an organized homeschool program, then these institutions will award the diploma according to their standards. If your child is homeschooled independently by you, then you have the option of issuing a diploma *if* your transcripts indicate that your child has met the necessary state requirements for graduation.

Your child has worked hard for twelve or so years; you definitely want to celebrate him or her with a diploma. A quick online search will result in many different companies who will print your official-looking, parent-issued diploma complete with your homeschool name and all the bells and whistles for a reasonable price.

Less is More

You do not need to put together a high school portfolio to send to colleges to try to impress them. Send only what they ask for. They don't want or need to see a lab report from tenth-grade biology or a persuasive essay about population control. However, portfolios are uber crucial for students who want to pursue a degree in fine arts, graphic design, interior design, art history, or any of the performing arts including music, dance, and theater. Again, review the admissions requirements for your desired program and plan for them accordingly.

Read for Pleasure

There is no list of must-reads. Your student will never need to send in a reading inventory for a college application. Let your child read what they want to in tandem with their coursework—as long as it's age appropriate, of course. Reading should not be a chore or a duty. It is better that they read as much as they want for pleasure than that they grow to hate reading and won't do it because they are forced to follow a designated list of prosaic and out-of-date classics that some administrator in an educational vacuum decided would be on the reading list for the last thirty years. Also, it is not necessary to read the classics for any reason except personal satisfaction. Books have the power to change your child's life in a magical and profound way; they can create a spark or light a fire within someone; encourage it.

My Child is the Best. Love, Mom

When you start the application process, you will soon find out that colleges typically prefer recommendations from teachers other than a child's mom. Imagine that! If I could write a letter of recommendation for my kid, it would probably make him sound like he had superpowers and was not only the smartest young adult on the planet but also the best at everything in the world. I'm just slightly biased.

To help solve this letter-of-recommendation dilemma, think of this: Has your child taken a class at a local community college or online? Have they had a coach, mentor, or volunteer coordinator that they might consider asking to write a recommendation on their behalf? Really this letter can come from anyone who can share insights into how your child might contribute to the academic, social, and cultural aspects of a college campus—

> **"**
>
> Give your child choices. It builds willpower and fuels initiative.
>
> LAURA KRONEN

anyone but you, that is. Policies on recommendation letters are different for most schools, so it's best to research your child's dream school and find out their individual requirements. I highly suggest you shelve the idea of yourself writing one.

chapter twelve

A Day In The Life

Whew! So now that you have some insight into what to include in your child's next twelve years, you might wonder how to structure your homeschool day to get done what needs to be done. When I talk to parents who are new to homeschooling, the question I get most frequently asked is, "How do you plan your day?" Having grown up with a traditional school background, the tendency is to plan each day like a regular school day. But the beauty of homeschooling is that you do not have to do this. Remember: Flexibility and individuality are the reasons you homeschool!

A primary consideration when planning your days is the ages of your brood. High schoolers will need significantly more structure in their day than younger children, and younger children will require substantially more hands-on attention than high schoolers.

The next scope of contemplation is how many days a week you want to homeschool. I have found that most parents decide on four to five days a week. Usually, four days is the perfect amount of time for little ones between four and six years old, and five days is perfect for older children. I have always schooled for all five days, but if I want to take a random day off because, as Marcia Brady once said, "Something suddenly came up," we do. At least once a month, we have something that gets in the way of homeschooling, but we never get worked up about it. *Don't sweat the small stuff* is the perfect idiom to live by when it comes to homeschooling. There is no hard and fast rule for when our school year begins and ends. The only requirement for my home state of Georgia is that a student gets 180 days of schooling each year. Make sure to check your state's specifications, if you haven't already any of the hundred other times I've mentioned it. I promise I do not nag this much in real life, but I want you to get off on the right foot!

> "
>
> Don't beat yourself up if you do not get around to "doing" school one day because you aren't feeling well or have to take care of other responsibilities.
> This is your school—
> you are the teacher AND the principal.
>
> LAURA KRONEN

Once you decide how many days you want to school, you need to choose your school calendar. Will you follow the calendar of the public school system? I have chosen to "kind of, sort of" do that. My kids do not get off for random holidays, but we will take an extra-long weekend to go on a spontaneous vacation without the slightest bit of guilt. We also do not take off for district-mandated "teacher workdays," which I have never entirely understood. I also will give them time off for the winter and spring breaks that the schools in my district have because many of their friends are off from school at that time and they want to hang out. Will you homeschool during the summer and offer up even more flexibility for fewer days per week and more breaks per year? That is a strong consideration for many. Kids spend most of the summer complaining that "they are bored" and begging for "something to do"; now you can give them something.

Knowing how long your kids will be in homeschool each year will help you plan your days and your lessons. Then, if you create your own course of study, you have carte blanche to carve out the exact schedule you want. Most curricula that you can purchase also offer a flexible schedule. However, some require online classes with live teachers, and those are mandatory for attendance—although just like traditional schools, you can be absent occasionally. Teachers are pretty flexible because they understand the very nature of homeschooling.

Regardless of the educational programming you choose, one of the most essential items in your arsenal will be a daily agenda. Each day I write plans for my children so that we all stay on task, accomplish what needs to be done, and I have a reference for the next day's assignments and lessons; the entire day is thought-out in detail. Plus, it serves as a great accountability tool for the kids as they check off what they have achieved throughout the day. I usually plan each day at a time, after my initial curriculum for the year is decided upon. If I tried to draft a calendar full of lessons, it would more than likely be trashed by week two of the year. Life never goes according to plan, so why should school? Some concepts are a breeze for my kid to understand, and we can move through lessons faster, and sometimes extra attention is needed in certain areas. So unless you want to use endless Wite-Out and erasers, I would consider doing the planning week by week, or even better, one day at a time.

This is my agenda-writing approach: every night from Sunday to Thursday, I sit down at my desk (the one I'm writing at right now), and I prepare the next day of school for my children. I'm going to be honest here; it's usually with a glass of wine or a vodka tonic in my hand because being a working homeschool mom is not easy, and my days are long! This planning process can take anywhere between a half hour and an hour, which will equate to one or two cocktails. From that starting point on Sunday night, I adjust for the remaining days of the week based on what we have accomplished each day. Admittedly, I am a little overzealous sometimes with what I think my kids can get done versus what they can actually get done, but we can always make accommodations because we are on OUR time. It's a beautiful thing.

I always use a basic notebook for our daily agendas, something with sturdy binding and thicker paper and at least ninety pages for the year. I write on both sides of the paper. I am a pencil-and-pen, tactile kind of person. I like to be able to hold the schedule and have my kids hold it too. Plus, it contains our entire educational history. For that reason, it is never, ever allowed out of the house, even for a sleepover at Grandma and Grandpa's. This is our bible of homeschooling, and it must be protected.

Bells and Whistles

Next, you need to decide what time you are going to begin

school each morning. You don't have to ring a bell or anything unless, of course, that's fun for you, but it is a good idea to have a specific time each morning to get the day started. My kids have an internal alarm clock that gets them up no later than eight a.m. I am not the sleep-in type and I think I have instilled that in my kids, too, but our schedules can be rearranged to accommodate the need for more sleep, especially when someone doesn't feel well, for those changing circadian rhythms of adolescence, or even for daylight savings time. They get up, get dressed, and then come downstairs, and we start with an overview of our day while we eat breakfast. I usually let them know what time I will be working with each of them independently during the day, but they know they have to be flexible because I also work, so I have quite a few balls in the air every day. Sometimes I might not get to Spanish instruction until *ocho de la noche*, but that's the nature of homeschooling in our house. The kids usually begin tackling their agendas with their independent work, mainly because I am not ready to dive into teaching until I get coffee and a workout in. Priorities.

When my boys complete assignments, they get graded, and I use Homeschool Minder (homeschoolminder.com) as a program to document their scores. There are many others available out there. Do your research and find out what works

> "
> Compulsory education suffocates a child's hunger to learn and instead engineers children and manipulates them into what the government wants them to be.
>
> LAURA KRONEN

best for you and your philosophy. Some programs are more complicated to use than others, and there is usually a fee for all of them. My biggest advice is to keep up with that weekly. If you fall behind, it can be pretty time-consuming, not to mention a pain in the neck, to catch up. And the more children you have, the exponentially harder it will be! Besides grade collection, there are many different places a record-keeping program can also help you stay organized, including attendance, lesson plans, student records, reading lists, and even keeping track of field trips. It will also generate a professional-looking transcript for you at the end of each year.

Substance Not Structure

So, I got a little sidetracked there. Let's get back to the layout of the day.

My kids will take a break around noon for lunch. They will eat and play video games for about forty-five minutes—Minecraft seems to have stood the test of time and has been a fan favorite year after year. I never have to tell my children to get back to their work, and that's one of the things that I appreciate most about homeschool. It has instilled an enormous sense of responsibility in my boys, and they know when they have to stop playing and get busy. They also know that I will not accept slacking off or shirking responsibilities. I'm very far from being a mean mommy, but I do expect a certain level of performance each day with schoolwork and with chores. However, my kids are free to roam around and take breaks whenever the need arises. Remember, at a traditional school they are asking children to sit still for hours a day without their minds wandering. This is preposterous. I do not even know an adult that can do that. It's just not natural.

That being said, when it's a beautiful day, I often bend my own rules, and we might take a more extended break to get outside, go for a walk, or ride bikes. My sons are really into motocross, sailing, airsoft, unicycling, and slacklining too. Really anything can be incorporated into our day, as we take advantage of opportunities as they arise, embrace the unexpected, and discover new adventures. This is typically when the real learning happens!

Hitting the Road

Expecting a child to learn only from a textbook is like asking them to look at a travel brochure and deeming it a vacation, so there are days that we might not "do" school at all and go on a field trip instead. We average two or three per month. Field trips have ranged from visiting an Amazon fulfillment center to see how a massive operation runs to touring a local recycling plant and learning about the process of collecting and processing

> "
> Kids need love, food, shelter, acceptance, support, and to be able to express themselves. They do not need formal schooling.
>
> LAURA KRONEN

materials and turning them into new products. We have visited an air traffic control tower, where we were informed about how controllers manage and keep flights safe around the country. We have tried mock cases at the Supreme Court and visited the

Margaret Mitchell House while reading *Gone with the Wind*. We listened to Kobie Boykins, the senior technical engineer at NASA and designer of the Mars rovers, speak at a symposium, and watched the government mint money at the Federal Reserve. Not going to lie, I had visions of the 2008 movie *Mad Money* running through my head as we did.

We learned about the many species of plants at the botanical gardens and immersed ourselves in space exploration at the Huntsville Space Center. We stepped foot on Fort Sumter, bicycled to where the Battle of Gettysburg took place, dedicated hours to the World War II Museum in New Orleans, and climbed aboard aircraft carriers in New York and descended into submarines in Charleston, South Carolina. We have visited the White House and the Air and Space Museum in Washington, DC. We have watched and actively participated in Shakespeare plays, attended the *Nutcracker* ballet, and visited dozens of other museums and historic sites.

We also have had the fortunate opportunity to go on grander field trips to places steeped in rich history, such as Vatican City to see the Sistine Chapel and other incredible works of art; the Colosseum, the Roman Forum, and the Pantheon in Rome; Pompeii to see an ancient world gone by; Venice to see the canals, Verona to see where *Romeo & Juliet* was set; Milan to see *The Last Supper*, Barcelona to practice our Spanish and to visit Park Güell and La Sagrada Familia; Mallorca to explore the caves; and a legion of other extraordinary adventures. Seeing an epic Michelangelo up close and in person, and learning about history while you are immersed in it, is incredibly different from reading about it in a textbook. Homeschooling affords us the possibility to take a trip when a golden opportunity arises and to not have to plot around traditional school breaks that usually result in hiked-up airfare, overbooked hotels, and crowded destinations.

Another perk is that there are no absentee notes to deal with. True story: when my son was attending public school in fifth grade, I once got a certified letter stating that I was going to be arrested for having my kid miss nine "unexcused" days of school while we were in Europe. I laughed and tossed it in my fireplace. Just try to arrest me, sunshine.

Traveling is incredible, but you don't have to leave the house to see the world. Explore famous landmarks all around the world, the halls of the greatest museums, and even leave this planet and take a tour of the International Space Station with virtual field trips. You can explore the vastest reaches of the world and enhance your child's learning experience right from your computer, and it will cost you nothing! Check out Trip Savvy (tripsavvy.com) for some fantastic and educational adventures.

Back to Business

I think I just took a field trip in my head from what I was talking about! Returning to outlining our homeschool day, yet again. The midday hours are when I work one on one with each child. I might have a PowerPoint prepared for a hard science concept, a book discussion for language arts, a review of a paper that they submitted at an earlier date, or a discussion of an endless array of topics. This is also the time I gauge how they have done with their assignments for the day, what concepts they are grasping or need additional help in, and how I will be preparing the next day's schedule.

Our typical day ends anywhere between three and five p.m., depending on when we start. And, to be candid, sometimes we don't get to everything I planned for the day, and that's OK. That's what tomorrow is for. I rarely, if ever, assign homework for my children, except reading, and they will usually do that at night before they go to bed. They read a chapter or two each evening of whatever book they are reading, which currently for my eighth grader is *1984* and for my eleventh grader is a biography about Canadian astronaut Chris Hadfield. The reason there is no other assigned homework is that we use our time during the day so efficiently and effectively. Even when we do not get to everything I had planned for the day, we still surpass, in leaps and bounds, the material that is learned in public school and in less time. It makes you wonder what the kids are doing held captive in those brick buildings all day long.

This all sounds like a piece of cake, right? Sometimes it is, but sometimes it's overwhelming. I have cried many days when I feel as though I am positively drowning in things to do and can't even fit taking a shower into my day. Lucky for me, dry shampoo exists and my hair looks good in a ponytail. The good news is that it's usually at the very beginning of each school year before we fall into the rhythm of our days and things get rolling. So, if that happens to you, don't worry—it will pass. Hang in there; it gets so much easier! But until then, wine helps.

Take it Slow

Homeschooling is not a race. The goal isn't to see how quickly a child can read, write, and count. Instead, it is a window of opportunity in life to spend time with your child and have them uncover knowledge and grow at their own pace.

For many families, homeschooling provides terrific opportunities to reflect on, reconsider, and restructure daily routines and rhythms around what matters most. Creating balance and carving out more time is an unintended byproduct of homeschooling. You can slow down, do things your way with intention and purpose. You can create routines and habits that will nourish you and your family. You can spend time exploring and following your passions, getting involved in community projects, minimizing stress, or trying something new. You can even take time to catch your breath, open yourself up to what "could be," and truly cherish your time with your children.

> "
>
> Help your child open up to the wonders of the world by asking intriguing questions: Why are there no more dinosaurs? Find the answers together.
>
> LAURA KRONEN

This is an education fueled by curiosity and creativity, by energy for learning and a spirit for living. Be creative! Does your daughter love music? Considering teaching literary elements around song lyrics. Does your son have an ant farm? Think about how to incorporate them into your biology lessons. Does your child want to ride a unicycle? There's your physical education class and a unique skill to master! Does your student love outer space? Create or look for lessons that feature rocket ships and planets. Does your son or daughter enjoy crafting? Make entrepreneurship a class and encourage them to start a small business selling their wares. The possibilities are endless!

Create Compassion

The ability to be heavily involved in our community and events is yet another advantage of homeschooling. Our homeschooling experience is infused with real-world community learning opportunities. Personal empowerment means realizing our potential to affect the world. We volunteer because we can and because it's a humbling, enriching experience. Giving back and serving others is what life is all about and is way more rewarding than meaningless busy work or constructing a shoebox diorama. Whether it be at a senior home, the Junior Achievement, church, the Red Cross, Thanksgiving food drives, city beautification projects, or shopping for Christmas gifts with underprivileged members of the community who need help, the ability to volunteer at a moment's notice is one of the greatest gifts we can give and homeschooling affords us that opportunity. As Mahatma Gandhi once said, "The best way to find yourself is to lose yourself in the service of others."[1]

Unschooling

I wasn't sure where to bring up *unschooling* because it doesn't fit neatly in any particular chapter, but it is worth bringing up because it is a term you often hear when you enter the homeschooling arena. When I first started homeschooling, I thought unschooling was the period of time in between leaving the traditional school system and starting homeschooling. Almost a deprogramming of sorts to recover from the artificial learning environment my kids were once in. I soon found out that the term for that is "deschooling" and is a time of convalescence that can take a few weeks to a few months depending on how much detox your child needs. When people are talking about unschooling, though, what they really mean is *natural, independent,* or *child-led* learning. It is not feasible to give unschooling directions for people to follow. Unschooling is an approach, not a method. It is a different way of looking at children and at life. It is based on the assumption that families will find the pathway that works best for them—without depending on the government, educational institutions, publishing companies, or self-acclaimed experts to tell them what to do. Unschooling does not mean that you do not teach anything at all to your child, or that children should figure it out on their own without the help and guidance of their parents. It just means that there is no adult force and control; parents should still actively participate in the development of their children.

A significant component of unschooling is grounded in doing real-world activities, not just because they are fundamentally engaging. There is an energy that derives from this that you can't purchase or weave into a curriculum. Children explore and figure things out all day long, and in an easygoing and encouraging home environment, "doing real things" ultimately brings about healthy mental development and valuable knowledge. It is entirely natural for children to read, write, play with numbers, learn about society, delve into the past, think, marvel, and do all those things that society attempts to forcibly place upon them in the traditional school environment.

Unschooling is an unmatched opportunity for each family

to do whatever makes sense for the growth, development, joy, and delight of their children. If you have a reason for using a curriculum and traditional school materials, you use them; if you don't, then you don't. If you want to watch videos to figure out how to do something, you can; if you want to learn how to do something just by attempting it, you can do that too. Simplicity. There is not a universally necessary or required component of unschooling either educationally or legally. Unschooling provides the opportunity to move away from traditional approaches of learning by teaching, and instead to develop independent ideas out of actual experiences, where the child is truly in pursuit of the knowledge, not force-fed it.

chapter thirteen

But What About Socialization?

This past year, my high school-aged son and I volunteered at a Junior Achievement Career Day for public school middle schoolers. During one part of the afternoon, I was speaking to a group of students. I was doing one of my child coaching seminars where I inspire kids, when thinking about what they "want to be when they grow up," to try making a career out of something they really enjoy doing. I then spoke individually to each child. I asked each student their name and to tell me something that they enjoyed doing. Out of the more than 150 kids that I asked, over the course of the day, 135 of them could not manage to have a conversation with me. They could not look me in the eye. They couldn't tell me what they enjoyed doing. At this moment, my eyes were opened to the future of the world, not just to what *my* children were going to be contributing, and I really started to worry. Only a tiny percentage of these students could manage to hold even a semblance of a conversation with my son or me. So, it makes me laugh when a public school mom, after telling her I homeschool, asks me the million-dollar question: "But what about socialization?!"

Although non-homeschoolers fear that homeschooling may turn our children into social misfits, we know that the opposite is correct and that *positive* socialization is one of the very best reasons to homeschool your children. *The International Encyclopedia of the Social & Behavioral Sciences* generally refers to socialization as the process of social influence through which a person acquires the culture or subculture of their group, and in the course of acquiring these cultural elements the individual's self and personality are shaped.[1]

Children require socialization with other children for them

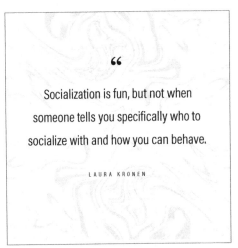

"

Socialization is fun, but not when someone tells you specifically who to socialize with and how you can behave.

LAURA KRONEN

to be productive members of society. I wholeheartedly agree, but, really, who wouldn't? If you have a child who is homeschooled and is rarely in public or interacting with others, you will have a problem with that child in years to come. That is just common sense and a pretty good bet that you will be

raising what will eventually become a socially awkward adult with the potential to be a serial killer one day. However, I have yet to meet a homeschooling family that does not socialize in *some* way. Does that mean they do not exist? No, but they certainly aren't the stereotypical norm. Homeschoolers know that their children need to interact with other children—of all age ranges, not just their own grade—and parents do everything possible to ensure their children receive this opportunity.

Socialization is meant to prepare children for the real world, which means learning to interact and deal with people from all walks of life; homeschooling actually does a superior job of this because homeschoolers spend more time out in society and not in a cement building, ostracizing other kids at the lunch table during the one time during the day they are "allowed to be social"—that is, if they weren't group-punished with a silent lunch. I cannot tell you how many times my children came home from elementary school and told me that happened. Ludicrous!

Contrary to decades of stereotypes painting homeschool students as awkward and antisocial, today's homeschoolers have far fewer difficulties in building healthy friendships than they did in the past. Not to mention, much of socialization these days starts on, moves to, or somehow involves the internet and social media, whether you are in a traditional school, homeschooled, on a desert island, or at the North Pole. Homeschooled children are taking part in the day-to-day routines of their towns and communities. They are definitely not isolated; in fact, they associate with all sorts of people, kids and adults. The classroom isn't the only place to make friends. Far from it.

Other forms of homeschool socialization come in the form of:

» team sports;

» co-ops (mentioned in an earlier chapter—groups of homeschoolers who get together to exchange different types of classes, allowing for socialization and taking advantage of the parents' individual teaching strong suits);

» support groups (homeschoolers that get together regularly for the children to play or participate in activities such as bowling, laser tag, and escape rooms);

» clubs such as 4-H, the Scouts, debate, and speech;

» music, dance, and drama lessons;

» field trip groups;

» and volunteering opportunities.

Most likely, many locations in your town such as public libraries, museums, community centers, and certain businesses offer programs and classes that cater to the growing number of homeschoolers. This allows for more avenues for education as well as opportunities for homeschooling families to get together. Socialization is a vital aspect of every child's life, and homeschool graduates that have been immersed in these avenues of socialization have shown just as much ability, if not more, to thrive in and contribute to society than their public school peers.

Homeschooling parents can take much of the credit for this. Homeschool moms and dads—at least, ones like me and my husband—have their kids long-term social development in mind, and they actively encourage their children to take advantage of social opportunities away from the house. As such, homeschooled children are obtaining all of the rules of behavior and systems of beliefs and attitudes that they need. They have good self-confidence and are likely to display fewer behavioral problems than other kids. They also tend to be more socially mature and have better leadership skills than other children of the same age. Recent studies from the NHERI show that adults who were home-educated are more politically tolerant than those who attended public school; they participate in local community service more frequently than the general population and go to and succeed at college at an equal or higher rate.[2] University of Arkansas researcher Albert Cheng compared the political tolerance of college students who had been homeschooled with that of those who had not. In the study, 304 students at a private Christian university were first asked to identify the social or political group whose beliefs were most strongly antithetical to their own. These students were then asked a series of questions to measure how politically tolerant they were of that group. The results showed that study participants who had been homeschooled before college were actually more politically liberal than those who had attended public schools. And the more years of homeschooling they had, the more politically tolerant they were.[3]

> "
> Any child that spends time with adults who are interested in the world and like to talk about it will learn far more than they ever will in a classroom with thirty other kids.
>
> LAURA KRONEN

Traditional schools are not conducive to socialization, and in fact, students are actually punished if they try to socialize in the classroom. The reality of traditional schools is that they are teaching students to be passive and submissive and to not stick up for themselves, which can follow the children throughout life.

Children can learn to take abuse, to ignore miserable bosses or abusive spouses later on. Kids with homeschooling educations develop self-confidence and self-esteem earlier, and they learn to deal with difficult people earlier in life. When they are ready to go out into the world, they know they have choices. And they choose wisely.

Socialization in homeschooling works better because children have more opportunities to be socialized through the modeling of proper social behavior by caring adults than through peers who do not know much more than they do and are many times the root of any problems that kids have. When kids are young and impressionable in a public school setting, it can be hard for their parents to tell which children to steer clear of if they do not know who their kids are hanging out with. Peer pressure comes into play here, and children want to mimic their peer group's behavior to fit in and receive group acceptance.

> "
> Introduce your children to interesting and capable people. Those will be the types of people they continue to seek out through life.
>
> LAURA KRONEN

Parents from all different educational platforms need to give their kids the skills they require to interact with others, and have the chance to protect their children. There are plenty of public school children that cannot communicate with anyone aside from kids in their own grade level, and that is using mostly acronyms and emojis. We have all seen children with no moral compass, no sense of right or wrong, and no respect for teachers and authority figures. The big question in homeschooling socialization is: "Who do we want our kids learning life skills from? Caring adults... or teachers who continually give out group punishments and peers who don't know any more than they do?"

But wait. There's a more significant, more looming, more pressing, more crucial question regarding socialization, and I get it all the time: "What about the prom?'"

OMG, the prom!!!!

Let's be completely honest here: Was your prom memorable? In a good way? I'm sorry, but prom is overrated. And if you are going to base your decision not to homeschool on one night/event that your child will miss out on, then perhaps you need to re-evaluate the reasons you want to homeschool in the first place. Would you rather your child miss out on one night or on an entire childhood of learning opportunities and experiences that are tailored specifically to that child?

Yeah, it's a Facebook memory for the parents, I totally get it. But truthfully, the pressure of the prom is kind of crazy these days. Have you seen some of these prom proposals? They are more elaborate than marriage proposals! The burden of coming up with something so outlandish combined with the pressure of being asked seems like overkill. But if you are really losing sleep over your child having that rite of passage, you can rest easy because many homeschool organizations and co-ops have established proms and graduations for homeschoolers, and many homeschoolers get invited to public school proms at local public schools through their friends. Boom! Prom drama solved. That said, I'm glad my kids think dances are outdated and lame (so do I) and have zero interest (thankfully) in ever going. And as an aside, if the prom is really that life-changing of an event, there are going to be hundreds of thousands of teens from 2020 that are scarred for their entire adult lives because they missed theirs due to the coronavirus quarantine.

So, as we've always known, there is no "socialization issue" in homeschooling. If anything, homeschoolers make a concentrated effort to seek out and engage in many social activities and, in many ways, have more opportunities for doing so than traditionally schooled children do. We do not have to do anything to socialize our children. Forced association is not socialization. Kids are born social. That's their nature. They will all figure it out.

chapter fourteen

12 Life Skills Every Kid Should Learn Sooner Rather Than Later

As parents, we protect our kids, albeit with the best of intentions, almost to the point of never letting them feel disappointment or sadness. We will do anything and everything to keep them safe and from hurting themselves, which many times seems like it can be a daily occurrence. I know the feeling of wanting to keep my boys in a protective bubble.

We "over-parent" them, thinking this will make them into perfect humans one day, but this can have the opposite effect on our kids and make them not ready to face the world as adults. By doing this, we deprive them of the chance to learn to manage their reactions and develop healthy coping mechanisms, and we may even prevent them from learning even the most basic of skills.

One day, they will find themselves in a place where no one is helping them out at every turn, and they will have to find their way in a cold, hard world that really doesn't care about them. I know it's a dark thought, but it's true. And if Mommy has been tending to every little need, even throughout their teenage life, they might find themselves unable to cope with even the smallest things. Moreover, teaching kids responsibility helps combat the arrogant entitlement attitude that has propelled it's way into the younger generations.

> "
> While communication is the most important life skill, there are still quite a few others that need to be mastered.
>
> LAURA KRONEN

One of the blessings of homeschooling is you can make everything a learning experience and anticipate more from your children with chores and family involvement since they are around the house more than they would be if they were attending traditional school eight hours a day. Another benefit is that necessary life skills are taught and mastered at an earlier age. Through trial and error I have come up with the twelve basic life skills that all kids should learn before they turn sixteen. These skills will benefit both them and you.

1. BE A SELF-STARTER. And this begins with getting up on their own. By the time a teen enters high school, he or she should be able to wake up on their own, brush their teeth, and get dressed in clean clothes without you having to guide them along on each step. If you are your teenager's alarm clock, you are sending the message that you'll always be here to wake them up, have food ready for them, and get them wherever they have to be on time no matter what. Many young adults have no concept of being accountable for time.

2. LEARN TIME MANAGEMENT. I have heard complaints from employers about recent college graduates entering the workforce and requiring a step-by-step playbook to complete even the most trivial task. Many of these young adults grew up in households where parents kept them on schedule and helicoptered over every task. Let's face it, many adults could still learn a few things about time management, but the more our children grasp how to manage their time before going off to college, the more successful they'll be. While parent involvement is undoubtedly beneficial to some extent, letting kids experience a bit of independence — and especially letting them figure a few things out on their own — will be a humongous long-term benefit.

3. MAKE A MEAL. SPAGHETTI COUNTS! Teach them how to boil an egg. Show them how to use the oven. Teaching kids how to cook also means setting them up for a healthier diet in the future. We need to eat every day, so this is an imperative skill for teens to know. Healthier meals are made at home and are much better than going through the drive-thru twice a day. Plus, home-cooked meals are usually less expensive. While the kids are at it, they should also learn to make a list and go food shopping to get the things they want to cook. And while they are eating what they cooked, they can learn the proper table manners to go along with it. (Sorry, that might have been three life skills lumped into one.)

4. PUMP GAS. I was pumping gas into the car the other day while my fourteen-year-old sat in the passenger seat playing

Fortnite when it dawned on me: What the heck? He should be pumping this gas. He's going to be learning to drive soon, and the mistake of putting diesel into an engine will not be one he will want to pay off on his own. Plus, it is teaching chivalry at the same time (and yes, I believe in it!).

5. BE THEIR OWN ADVOCATE. You've heard stories about parents calling college professors to complain about a grade, right? That's *not* OK. After junior high, if you're the parent that is continually emailing the teacher, you are teaching your kid that they are not capable enough to handle any issues themselves. Kids need to recognize that they have the right to let their voices be heard respectfully. Teach your child how to have a discussion with someone in a position of authority and to advocate for themselves. For example, if they oppose a grade received at school, urge them to speak to their teacher respectfully and to get clarification or a chance to make corrections while at the same time being able to accept criticism. So many kids cannot take critique because their moms have told them how they can do no wrong their entire lives.

6. PACK THEIR OWN (SCHOOL, OVERNIGHT, VACATION) BAG. *raising hand* I was guilty of not doing this for sure. It was easier for me to do it than to have my child pack half of what he needed. One day that overnight bag becomes a briefcase, though, and if they haven't learned that skill of being responsible for remembering their own stuff, they will be that person that is always forgetting things. Even packing for a trip should be a life skill that a child should be comfortable with by the time they enter high school. If you don't trust them enough to pick out the clothing that will look good for a major event or party (and I'm definitely with you on that), at least have them make a list of the things they need to wear or go away with.

7. DO LAUNDRY. One day, after coming back from the pool, I told my elementary-aged kids to put their wet bathing suits into the washer, and I went downstairs later to find them in the dryer. Red flag! Do you know which one is the washing machine, boys? I can do laundry in my sleep, but it wasn't always that way. I ruined many a white shirt by mixing something red in with it. Save them the trouble of that happening and instead

> **"**
> You need life skills to recognize opportunity.
>
> LAURA KRONEN

show them the way, watch them do it on their own once or twice to make sure they've got it, and then let them handle it on their own. Same thing with dishwasher duties.

8. ORDER OFF THE MENU THEMSELVES. Sounds pretty basic, but I'm guessing that you probably talk to your kids about what they want to eat, then order it for them. Have them get comfortable with ordering their own food.

9. TEACH THEM ABOUT MONEY. It could literally make or break your kid's success as an adult. Once your son or daughter is old enough to earn an allowance, they're also old enough to begin obtaining financial skills and managing money. This is an excellent time to teach them to wait before they buy something and to know the difference between wants and needs. Although I have a hard time deciphering that myself. I'm really not sure if lip gloss, shoes, and wine are wants or needs for me. Anyway, teach them to comparison shop when you're at the store or shopping online together. Teens can start learning about building credit, handling debt, and investing for future goals. Just as a postscript, I do not believe in allowance. I do not think my kids should be paid for helping out around the house. I do believe in rewards, though if you really want something badly enough, then you are going to figure out how to go above and beyond to earn it.

10. HOW TO TALK TO STRANGERS. "Don't talk to strangers" is not always a good lesson. Instead, teaching children how to tell the difference between the creepy people and the "everyday strangers" that they might encounter is a better one. Great example: I was bicycling through the greenway one morning when a copperhead snake slithered out right in front of me, and I froze in my tracks. At the same time, a little girl was bicycling toward the snake and me. Her parents were walking a few hundred yards behind her, and she was not even in their field of vision. I calmly shouted to the girl to stop pedaling and back up her bicycle because there was a poisonous snake in front of me, and her response was to ignore me. Then I was much more stern in my command, and I think I might have scared her, but I surely saved her from being bitten. When her parents finally made it to where we were, they apologized and said that their daughter had ignored me as they have taught her not to talk to strangers. We and our children currently live in a world of silent communication. Complete conversations take place over text and social media posts, so it's up to us to verbally engage and connect with our kids. Personal communication skills are lacking in so many children these days. Try to get one to look you in the eye when they speak to you. Teaching them to communicate face to face (and I don't mean on FaceTime!) will go a long way. Out in the world, our kids will come across many strangers daily, and our children need to know how to clearly

" Life skill phrases to live by: let it go, ignore them, give it time, don't compare, stay calm.

LAURA KRONEN

communicate with them. But if children have never been encouraged to speak to strangers on their own, and if their parents have always spoken for them, a child's communication skills will be compromised.

11. HOW TO HANDLE DISAPPOINTMENT. I know failure is rough. And to see your kid fail? Even tougher. But as challenging as it is to sit on your hands and keep your mouth quiet as your kid makes mistakes, failure teaches big lessons. And kids who have never had to deal with failure find themselves unable to cope as adults when a relationship goes wrong or a work project doesn't pan out. So you don't make the cheerleading squad. Too bad. If you want it, practice harder. Got cut from the basketball team? Well, maybe you aren't cut out for basketball.

What you don't want to do is create a world where discipline and accountability no longer exists. You know what I'm talking about. All this swooping in and fixing whatever "injustice" you feel was committed against your child creates socially handicapped children that have no clue how to get through life without an adult there to fight for something they did not earn or deserve. That's it. I'm stepping off of my soapbox now.

12. SHOWING UP AND WORKING HARD. While showing up is the first step toward attaining a goal, children must learn the relevance of putting in the labor to actually reach the goal. Remember that unearned rewards set children up to expect a win just for showing up, resulting in entitlement. This everyone-gets-a-trophy thing has got to stop. Congratulations, you came in twenty-sixth place. Here's your trophy! This isn't how the world works. Ever see that in the Olympics? What about the World Series? American Idol? No, you are booted off and forgotten about if you didn't place in the top three. And that very lesson makes those that are genuinely driven work even harder!

Of course there are many more life skills to master before our children go off to live their lives on their own, but the more we can prepare them for what life will be like when they aren't living in our house, the more successful they will be! Adulting has enough of a learning curve and having the basics down will help make everything else go a little bit smoother. Lastly, remember to be a good example. Even if you do not think your children are always *listening*, they are always *watching*.

What Homeschooling Is Missing

I will voluntarily admit that my children have missed out on some things because we homeschooled. Undoubtedly that there are many experiences that public school provides that we just cannot duplicate in our home. Some people even quit homeschooling when they get to the middle and high school levels because they are worried their children will miss out, although there are so many ways to fill those recesses.

Keeping an Eye on the Ball

In my home state of Georgia, students are not allowed to participate in public school sports unless they are actually enrolled at the school for a certain amount of hours every week. Well, that sort of rules out us homeschoolers, doesn't it? Not every state has that rule, but for those who do, there are various sports that homeschoolers can take part in. Many towns offer recreational leagues for sports such as lacrosse, soccer, baseball, and football. Many of these programs allow kids to play straight through middle school.

Another thing to consider is individual sports instead of team sports, sports like swimming, tennis (my favorite), karate, golf, or gymnastics. You can find most of these available through private lessons, a local gym, or your local YMCA. I can't say this is a particularly pressing issue for my family, though, because my children are more academic and artistic than sporty and competitive. Still, for some, this might pose a problem. That said, I'm a major advocate of homeschoolers *not* using the public schools for anything even if it is allowed. I think staying as far away from the schools as possible is the ideal.

The Show Must Go On

My son is a vocalist and a musician that plays bass and guitar. To work on and showcase his talents, he needs to take private lessons instead of music lessons within the public school. He does not get to participate in chorus or band, and we do not get to go to these free school performances. However, he takes individual voice and guitar lessons and has incredible showcases where he performs solo in front of packed audiences. He is also in a rock band that plays all over the state at local festivals and events.

> "
>
> Homeschooling is not just an act of liberation. It is an act of commitment and passion for creating an awareness of life while guiding our children to become healthy, curious, and independent adults.
>
> LAURA KRONEN

What about theater? How can a homeschooled kid ever star in *Annie*? This dilemma is easily solved with an internet search for local theater groups, and most of the children in those theater companies are way more serious and into it than those in the after-school club. You also might find a summer music or theater camp in your area.

State of the Art

One of the (many) things I took issue with when my children were in public school was the methods used in art class. Every student was shown the same piece of art—in this case, a Georgia O'Keeffe flower—and they were instructed to copy it. I found this to be so bizarre; in the only subject that they got to have a creative outlet, they all had to paint the *exact same* red flower.

So, while I am not trained in the arts, do not have incredible artistic ability, and am definitely not a DIYer, I *do* have a creative mindset. My children and I come up with different art projects to experiment with every few days. When we first started this practice, they were thrilled that they had free rein to let their inventive minds loose. Together we would try out all different mediums and learn about different genres of art. Then they got to focus on and develop their skills in the areas they enjoyed most.

Most co-ops will offer fine arts classes because it is a subject that sometimes gets ignored in homeschool. Many parents think because they can only draw a stick figure that they cannot teach art. If you don't have a co-op in your area or don't want to join one (like I didn't), look around for an art studio in your town or perhaps an art instructor that offers individual art classes to kids, or just spend a few moments perusing Pinterest for ideas. My older son also took an art history class while dually enrolled, and my middle schooler took it alongside him. Two kids with one stone!

The University of Life

I know I spoke about this earlier, but it's worth bringing up again here. Homeschoolers certainly do not miss out on field trips. I'd say that homeschoolers are renowned for taking field trips, but outsiders think differently. Yes, for sure, they miss out on having to get all those permission slips signed, riding the hot school bus to the location, and being hustled through the venue for a few hours with a couple hundred other kids for their one big, exciting day off of the school property each year. There's not much learning that goes on during these public school field trips. For those students, it's a day out of dodge. Meanwhile, homeschoolers get to select their own field trips based on their interests and what they are studying. They get to decide how long they will stay and what they want to spend more time doing. They get to fully experience and enjoy the trip because they can go during less crowded times. All of these benefits add up to a much more enjoyable experience.

> "
> Most learning is not the result of instruction; it is the result of actively participating in the activity. You do not learn to walk by following the rules. You learn to walk by figuring it out on your own and falling down a few times.
>
> LAURA KRONEN

The Graduate

Homeschooled kids might miss out on a big, elaborate ceremony at graduation, but they don't have to. Many homeschool organizations, some co-ops, and even some churches will put on a yearly graduation ceremony for graduating homeschoolers.

You can even get your child a cap and gown and set up a graduation celebration at your own house; creative examples of that were in abundance on Facebook throughout our spring 2020 quarantine.

Join the Club, Maybe

The crux of the matter is, most homeschoolers *will* miss out on activities and opportunities such as writing for the school paper, being on the yearbook committee, and participating in student council. However, if these things are significant to you and your family, you can still make them happen. Again, look into your local co-ops or even community newspapers and see if they offer any of these opportunities; there is a good chance they do.

Honor Thy Self

My son will not get those extra ten points added to his AP course's final grade point average (GPA) or the extra five points supplemented for honors because I am not an accredited institution that the College Board approves of. So, my child will never have higher than a 4.0 GPA, despite him taking those same courses with me and regardless of the fact that he scored all 4's and 5's on his AP tests. I admit I felt regret about that for a little while. He is a smart kid and deserves to be looked at competitively with the other kids who took the same course. However, he is still getting the same college credit for that course that any traditional school student will get. The exception is that my son didn't have the stress of hours upon hours of homework, and he went at his own pace. Frankly, he learned more than most students because we covered *everything,* not just what we were able to get to. That is why he did so well. He was done entirely with "learning" by April 1 and had six weeks to study for the mid-May exam.

In every case, my children have conquered the supposed "missed opportunity" and have not been significantly affected by not having these experiences at the public school. Homeschool kids don't miss out; their schooling and life just looks a little different from the others. But what fun would life be if everyone and all of their experiences were the same?

The Joy of Missing Out

But wait, there's more. Let's not forget these other missed opportunities that my children had because they were homeschooled:

- » Opportunities to purchase drugs or drink alcohol.

- » Opportunities to have inappropriate conversations regarding sex.

- » Opportunities to spend more time with friends than family.

Often, when kids go to school for eight hours a day, school becomes their life. Their friends become more important than their family, and their family just becomes a group of autonomous people all residing in the same house. Homeschooling removes or significantly lessens the negative factors of adolescence and increases the positives. It's clear to see that my children have *not* missed out on anything significant because we homeschool. With a little resourcefulness, we can find ways to ensure what our children truly need and want, so that they pursue what interests them because they have the time to do so. You just need to remind yourself why you started this and what your ultimate goals are when it comes to your child's education.

Your kids might miss out on some things, but so might their public school peers—like a close-knit family, great meals, sleeping in, no homework, awesome field trips, and an individualized, enriching education.

> **"**
>
> Trust yourself,
> trust your children,
> trust the process.
>
> LAURA KRONEN

chapter sixteen

How To Avoid Homeschool Burnout

Mother, teacher, nurse, chef, social director, chauffeur, boss babe. How do you do it all and still stay sane? You might be homeschooling your kids, and yes, that is an important aspect of your life once you resolve to homeschool, but when you place all of your other hats on, and maybe even throw a career on top of the pile, when and how do you take care of YOU?

Homeschooling moms are the first ones up in the morning and the last ones to bed at night. They always seem to be putting themselves after everyone else. But there comes a time in every homeschooling mom's life that she has to commit to self-care. That time is now. However, finding the time to get started with personal care can be challenging. Even so, we all need a little "me" time in our lives so that we do not feel that we are always living our lives for someone else.

If you are asking yourself, "What is me time?" then you clearly need it. Simply stated, it's any moment in time that is dedicated to *your* happiness. Food shopping sans children is *not* me time. Running all over town to pick up supplies for your child's science project is *not* me time. Taking a shower is *not* me time. Giving yourself a facial, reading a book, meditating, praying, browsing the aisles of Sephora (alone)—those are all "me" time activities. Unless your child touching every eyeshadow and lipstick in the place is your idea of a good time. As long as you enjoy what you are doing and it benefits *just* you, it can be considered "me" time.

The Mother Lode

It's incredible how often I hear of moms who are feeling burnt out, stressed, or who are convinced that they aren't measuring up. And believe me, I get it. Feeling regular bouts of overload seems to be a rite of passage for homeschool moms. We often don't think that we're doing enough unless our plates are entirely full; if they aren't, we must be doing something wrong. We tend to push ourselves until we reach the breaking point. Surprisingly, burnt-out women don't make the best caregivers. They also can get pretty snappy, short, weepy, and downright angry. You must find a way to put the oxygen mask on yourself first so that you will also be able to take care of others around you.

> "
> There are not always enough hours in the day to teach children and to work, clean, cook, and get everything else done. I'd rather hire out the cleaning than my children's learning any day of the week.
>
> LAURA KRONEN

These simple tips will help you to stay present, stay healthy, and remain bulletproof.

» **RENEW AND RECHARGE** – With a little bit of advanced planning and ingenuity, you can find ways to get some time to yourself throughout the week. Take a bath, read a book, put on a mask, and listen to music. Don't forget to use the smelly bath salts and candles to set the mood for chillaxing. Even if you get to soak for fifteen minutes, it will help you to relax and recharge.

» **FOCUS ON THE GOOD** – Many times, we are so focused on the negative aspects of our lives that we do not recognize the incredible things which are all around us. When you pause and start going over them in your head, you will soon feel more blessed than stressed.

» **ASK FOR HELP WHEN YOU NEED IT** – No one expects you to do everything on your own, but they also can't guess what you are thinking. Don't be shy; ask for help. Also, there may be subjects that you may need help teaching, and that's okay. It's okay to hire someone to tutor your child or to have your child take an external class in a subject that you aren't at ease with teaching.

» **TAKE THE DAY OFF FROM TEACHING** – Homeschooling can take a toll on a mom really fast. This is why you need to plan vacation days from teaching. It's okay to let some things go. Really, it is.

» **LEARN TO SAY NO** – We cannot do everything that is expected of us without pushing our limits. Learning to say no to the many requests may be an obvious time management tip for anyone, but that doesn't make it an easy thing to do. Moms encounter many requests and demands for their help, time, and attention, and we fear that saying no will often upset someone. What we don't always understand is that when we say yes too often, people also get disappointed because we are spread too thin and small details end up slipping through the cracks. That's why it is crucial to look at your priorities and learn to say no to time demands that aren't absolutely necessary. The more you say no, the more found time you will have.

» **GET ORGANIZED** – An ounce of prevention is worth a pound of cure. Simply being organized can eliminate the stress that homeschooling moms face every day. Keep an organizer, use your smartphone for one of the reasons it was intended, and plan ahead so that you aren't scrambling at the last second.

» **DELEGATE RESPONSIBILITIES** – Yes, when your next of kin come to you, they are so sweet and helpless that you end up doing everything for them, and these habits are difficult to break. But it is nearly impossible for one frazzled person to do it all. You are going to snap eventually. While it's tempting to do all the household chores and responsibilities yourself—most of us are guilty of this because we know the *right* way to do everything— putting some effort into getting the rest of the family to contribute will pay off in spades in the long run. Break chores down into smaller, easily digestible tasks and then reward people for doing them. Even if the kids don't make the bed the same way as you do, as hard as it is, just leave it be and shut the door.

» **TAKE SHORTCUTS** – I am a perfectionist, so I know how hard it is to just settle for a *good-enough* job, but if you can get frozen vegetables or canned sauce for dinner, do it. Doctor them up if you have to. If you can afford a dishwasher that can handle unrinsed dishes, even better. It doesn't make you a bad mom. Find the shortest, most efficient route to where you need to go, whether it's getting to the office, getting schoolwork done, or getting the house clean, and take it.

> **"**
> You will have good days.
> You will have great days.
> You will have bad days.
> You will have awful days.
> It is all part of the package.
>
> LAURA KRONEN

» **KEEP PRIORITIES REALISTIC** – Even though making the decision to homeschool your children is a noble one, it also comes with pressing issues that you will need to overcome including time management and potential work responsibilities. Realize this when planning and establishing your homeschool schedule. Do not overpromise to yourself; the chances are higher you will underdeliver.

» **BE FLEXIBLE** – Is your life turned upside down when your day doesn't go as planned? While it's essential to have an idea of how you'd like your daily existence to look, it's important to be flexible enough to accommodate the unexpected things that moms encounter, like a sick kid, spilled milk, or lunatic meltdowns while out at the store. (By the way, every child has had a meltdown at some point or another—no one is paying too much attention to yours.) Having a rhythm for your day but adding in time cushion and backup plans can help. Take the stress out of the unforeseen and keep one schedule setback from screwing up your whole day or week.

» **LEARN TO MOVE ON** – No matter what trials or tribulations we are currently experiencing, we can let go of the hurt, the pain, and the fear, and choose a positive attitude.

» **TAKE TIME TO REST** – You will feel tired on occasion; however, if you find yourself tired *all of the time* or just plain exhausted, then things have to change. Make sure you go to the doctor. Get a physical. Take vitamins. Drink more water. Get out into the sunshine. Vitamin D is a cure-all for so many things. Spending time outdoors can help you reduce stress, lower your blood pressure, and be more mindful. Getting fresh air can help reduce fatigue, making it a great way to overcome symptoms of depression or burnout.[1] Spending time alfresco can also help you sleep better at night, especially if you do some physical activity, like hiking or walking.

» **PRACTICE THANKFULNESS** – Meditate. I can't do it, but

maybe you can. There are some easy-to-find, calming apps for that. What I do instead is, every time I see the clock on my phone turn to 11:11 or 1:11, I take a one-minute pause and thank God for everything I have. I see it every single day, and although one might say I am looking at my phone too much, I believe it's a sign to slow down and be grateful for what I have and what really matters.

» **TAKE IT SLOW** – Make small, daily changes towards your goals, and watch them add up and transform your life over time.

» **NEVER COMPARE YOURSELF** – Moms often end up feeling discouraged because we think that everyone else has smarter kids, cleaner homes, better bodies, more money, and a better life. Do not get stuck in the comparison trap. You will never measure up when you are comparing your day-to-day life to someone else's highlight reel.

» **DO NOT FORCE YOUR CHILDREN TO BE SOMETHING THEY ARE NOT** – Stop trying to put a square peg in a round hole. We need to stop trying to force our children into the kind of people we want them to be. Instead, we need to be a model for them to follow.

» **FIND BALANCE** – Yes, you are Superwoman, but you can't do it all if you expect to maintain your sanity. Instead, save the world one task at a time.

» **DON'T EXPECT PERFECTION** – Expecting perfection

puts unnecessary stress on your family. The beginning stages of homeschooling are trial and error, and you need to give yourself some slack. Being a perfectionist myself, this tip is challenging for me to follow, but oh so necessary.

» **AVOID OVER-SCHEDULING** – When we don't have downtime, it's easy to wear ourselves out. I have learned to keep my early mornings quiet and to try to leave some evenings during the week free to just be home instead of running around. I'll say it again: *Don't over-schedule*.

» **MAKE SLEEP A PRIORITY** – Seriously. Sleep can have a considerable effect on how you feel, both emotionally and physically. Not only for you but for your children too. Establish a set bedtime for your children and one for yourself while you are at it. Give yourself time to wind down. Watch a television show or, better yet, turn off the electronics. Chill.

» **TAKE CARE OF YOUR SKIN** – When we were teens, we were obsessed with skincare, but the busier we became, things started to slide. Being an Ivory soap and water kind of girl isn't the best thing for your skin. You don't have to spend a fortune on products, but allow yourself the luxury every night of having a skincare ritual. Your future self will thank you.

» **DRINK YOUR WATER** – Buy yourself a pretty, reusable water flask, and drink your water every day. If you consume coffee and wine (by now you have figured out

I do), you'll need even more water. Set a goal of at least forty-eight ounces every day. Or forty. Or even thirty-six. Whatever you feel you can stick to, and then maybe you can increase it over time. Just drink some darn water!

» **GET SOME EXERCISE** – You have heard it before, exercise is good for us, both physically and mentally. It boosts your mood and reduces stress and anxiety, not to mention that it helps you shed extra pounds. Even a fifteen-minute walk every day will do you, your mind, and your body good. Create a routine that works for you.

> **"**
> Trust yourself,
> trust your children,
> trust the process.
>
> LAURA KRONEN

» **EAT RIGHT** – The food we eat will keep us healthy or contribute to weight gain and diseases such as diabetes, but it can also keep our minds working and alert. Eating the right foods can help prevent short-term memory loss and inflammation, both of which can have long-term effects on the brain and, in turn, the rest of the body.

» **DON'T FEEL GUILTY** – I have heard homeschool moms talk about the guilt they feel because they get to the end of the school year, and they only have completed 178 school days instead of 180. Or the guilt they felt when they didn't get to go on a field trip because a child was sick. Or when they fell short of completing the suggested curriculum during a fall semester. Or even when they didn't get to teach math one Thursday. It is time to let the guilt go. Let it go!

Believe it or not, your children will grow up someday, and knowing that *you* were the one who taught them not just their ABC's but literally a million other things will give you a sense of pride that is unmatched. What's more, the memories you will get to cherish because you actually spent your child's *childhood* with them are priceless.

You're as ready as you'll ever be. Everything leading up to this moment has prepared for everything you will do now and in the years to come. What you're not ready for, you will become ready for. You might fail at some things. But guess what? You will survive. You will learn to use failures as momentum, and the insight you gain will lead you to success.

Life will never introduce something to you that you won't be able to figure out. You are ready. You can do this!

References And Sources

FOREWORD

1. Blankley, B. (2020, May 15). Poll: 40 percent of Americans more likely to home-school, enroll children in virtual schools after lockdown. Retrieved June 07, 2020, from https://www.thecentersquare.com/national/poll-40-per-cent-of-americans-more-likely-to-home-school-enroll-children-in-virtual-schools/article_5fd3578c-96ac-11ea-92b0-97ff4de081e9.html

CHAPTER ONE

1. Brian Ray, "Research Facts on Homeschooling," National Home Education Research Institute, January 6, 2015, https://files.eric.ed.gov/fulltext/ED556234.pdf.

2. Public Affairs. (2019, December 05). What Is Bullying. Retrieved June 09, 2020, from https://www.stopbullying.gov/bullying/what-is-bullying

3. "Facts About Bullying," U.S. Department of Health and Human Services, June 10, 2019, www.stopbullying.gov/resources/facts.

4. Teen Substance Use & Risks. (2020, February 10). Retrieved June 09, 2020, from https://www.cdc.gov/ncbddd/fasd/features/teen-substance-use.html

5. Learning from Student Voice: College and Career Readiness. (n.d.). Retrieved June 09, 2020, from https://youthtruthsurvey.org/college-and-career-readiness/

6. Weller, C. (2018, January 21). Homeschooling could be the smartest way to teach kids in the 21st century - here are 5 reasons why. Retrieved June 09, 2020, from https://www.businessinsider.com/reasons-homeschooling-is-the-smartest-way-to-teach-kids-today-2018-1

7. African American Homeschool Parents' Motivations for Homeschooling and Their Black Children's Academic Achievement. (n.d.). Retrieved June 09, 2020, from https://www.tandfonline.com/doi/abs/10.1080/15582159.2015.998966

8. Homeschooling: The Research, Scholarly articles, studies, facts, research. (2020, May 22). Retrieved June 09, 2020, from https://www.nheri.org/research-facts-on-homeschooling/

9. Masci, D. (2016, January 08). Why Millennials are less religious than older Americans. Retrieved June 09, 2020, from https://www.pewresearch.org/fact-tank/2016/01/08/qa-why-millennials-are-less-religious-than-older-americans/

10. Connection Between Religion and Homeschooling. (2015, October 08). Retrieved June 10, 2020, from https://www.ulc. org/ulc-blog/connection-religion-homeschooling

11. Huseman, J. (2015, February 17). Why More and More Black Families Are Homeschooling Their Children. Retrieved June 10, 2020, from https:// www.theatlantic.com/education/archive/2015/02/ the-rise-of-homeschooling-among-black-families/385543/

12. Sun, L. (2018, October 11). Percentage of young U.S. children who don't receive any vaccines has quadrupled since 2001. Retrieved June 10, 2020, from https://www.washingtonpost. com/national/health-science/percentage-of-young-us-children-who-dont-receive-any-vaccines-has-quadrupled-since-2001/2018/10/11/4a9cca98-cd0d-11e8-920f-dd52e-1ae4570_story.html

13. Six common misconceptions about immunization. (2013, February 19). Retrieved June 10, 2020, from https://www. who.int/vaccine_safety/initiative/detection/immuniza-tion_misconceptions/en/index4.html

14. What Happens When We Don't Vaccinate? (n.d.). Retrieved June 10, 2020, from http://www.pkids.org/immunizations/ vaccines_safe_choice/consequences_not_vaccinating.html

15. Why Are Teachers Mostly Liberal? - Pacific Research Institute. (n.d.). Retrieved June 10, 2020, from https://www. pacificresearch.org/why-are-teachers-mostly-liberal/

16. National Jewish Health. (2016, March 07). Study: Homeschool Students Sleep Better. Retrieved June 10, 2020, from https://www.nationaljewish.org/about/news/ press-releases/2016/homeschool-sleep

17. Sleep for Teenagers. (2020, June 01). Retrieved June 10, 2020, from https://www.sleepfoundation.org/articles/teens-and-sleep

18. Hagenauer, M., Perryman, J., Lee, T., & Carskadon, M. (2009). Adolescent changes in the homeostatic and circadian regulation of sleep. Retrieved June 10, 2020, from https://www.ncbi.nlm.nih.gov/pmc/articles/PMC2820578/

19. Homeschooling: The Research, Scholarly articles, studies, facts, research. (2020, May 22). Retrieved June 10, 2020, from https://www.nheri.org/research-facts-on-homeschooling/

CHAPTER TWO

1. DeSilver, Drew. "U.S. Academic Achievement Lags That of Many Other Countries." , Pew Research Center, 15 Feb. 2017, www.pewresearch.org/fact-tank/2017/02/15/u-s-students-internationally-math-science/.

2. "U.S. Students from Educated Families Lag in International Tests." Education Next, 10 Mar. 2016, www.educationnext.org/us-students-educated-families-lag-international-tests/.

3. Governing. Education Spending Per Student by State, www.governing.com/gov-data/education-data/state-education-spending-per-pupil-data.html.

4. Grace Chen, "10 Advantages to Public Education," Public School Review, May 25, 2020, www.publicschoolreview.com/blog/10-advantages-to-public-education.

5. O'Donnell, Erin. "The Risks of Homeschooling." Harvard Magazine, 1 June 2020, www.harvardmagazine.com/2020/05/right-now-risks-homeschooling.

6. O'Donnell, "The Risks of Homeschooling."

7. O'Donnell, "The Risks of Homeschooling."

8. Bartholet, Elizabeth. "Homeschooling: Parent Rights Absolutism vs. Child Rights to Education & Protection." SSRN Electronic Journal, 2019, doi:10.2139/ssrn.3391331.

CHAPTER THREE

1. Medlin, Richard G. "Homeschooling and the Question of Socialization Revisited." Peabody Journal of Education, vol. 88, no. 3, 2013, pp. 284–297., doi:10.1080/016195 6x.2013.796825.

2. Weller, Chris. "Americans Are Rejecting the 'Homeschool Myth' - and Experts Say the Misunderstood Education Might Be Better than Public or Charter Schools." Business Insider, Business Insider, 23 Jan. 2017, www.businessinsider. com/homeschooing-more-popular-than-ever-2017-1.

3. "Home-Schooled Teens Ripe for College." U.S. News & World Report, U.S. News & World Report, www.usnews. com/education/high-schools/articles/2012/06/01/ home-schooled-teens-ripe-for-college.

4. White-Cain, Paula. "Your Future Is Found in Your Daily Routine. Successful People Do Daily What Others Do Occasionally!! #Future #Success." Twitter, Twitter, 25 Jan. 2014, twitter.com/Paula_White/status/427225443268194304.

5. Daskal, Lolly. "18 Effective Habits of Highly Successful People." Inc.com, Inc., 2 Feb. 2017, www.inc.com/lolly-das- kal/18-effective-habits-of-highly-successful-people.html.

CHAPTER FIVE

1.	STUDY.COM, study.com/academy/popular/how-much-does-it-cost-to-homeschool.html.

CHAPTER SIX

1.	"#MetKids," Metropolitan Museum of Art, 2020, www.metmuseum.org/art/ online-features/metkids/.

CHAPTER EIGHT

1.	"AP vs. CLEP ~ What's the Difference? Which Is Right for You?" Credits Before College, 24 Nov. 2018, creditsbeforecollege.com/ap-vs-clep/.

2.	"Learn About the College-Level Examination Program (CLEP): College Planning." Learn About the College-Level Examination Program (CLEP) | College Planning, bigfuture.collegeboard.org/get-in/testing/learn-about-the-clep-program.

3.	"Search Institution Policies – CLEP – The College Board." CLEP, 23 Aug. 2018, clep.collegeboard.org/school-policy-search.

4.	"AP Score Distributions." AP Score Distributions – AP Students | College Board, apstudents.collegeboard.org/about-ap-scores/score-distributions.

CHAPTER NINE

1. "Development Process." Development Process | Common Core State Standards Initiative, www.corestandards.org/about-the-standards/development-process/.

2. Mahoney, Emily, et al. "Florida Gives Common Core a Failing Grade, Announces New State School Standards." Miamiherald, Miami Herald, www.miamiherald.com/news/local/education/article239590948.html.

3. STUDY.COM, study.com/academy/goal/transferable-credit.html.

CHAPTER TEN

1. Giebel, Kiley, et al. "15 Reasons Why Standardized Tests Are Worthless." The American Institute for Learning and Human Development, www.institute4learning.com/2013/02/28/15-reasons-why-standardized-tests-are-worthless-2/.

2. Giebel, "15 Reasons Why Standardized Tests Are Worthless."

3. Giebel, "15 Reasons Why Standardized Tests Are Worthless."

4. "Test Anxiety (for Kids) - Nemours KidsHealth." Edited by Kathryn Hoffses, KidsHealth, The Nemours Foundation, July 2018, kidshealth.org/en/kids/test-anxiety.html.

5. Petersen, Ella. "Standardized Tests." Science Leadership Academy @ Center City, scienceleadership.org/blog/standardized_tests.

6. ASCD Guest Blogger, et al. "15 Reasons Why Standardized Tests Are Problematic." ASCD

Inservice, 14 June 2018, inservice.ascd. org/15-reasons-why-standardized-tests-are-problematic/.

7. "How Much Weight Does the SAT Carry in an Application?" Manhattan Review, 16 Apr. 2020, www.manhattanreview. com/sat-role-in-college-application/.

8. https://www.amazon.com/Defending-Standardized-Testing-Richard-Phelps/ dp/0805849122

9. "Pros & Cons - ProCon.org." Standardized Tests, 5 June 2020, standardizedtests.procon.org/.

10. Elliott, Philip. "Standardized Tests Popular with Parents, Poll Shows." Spokesman.com, The Spokesman-Review, 18 Aug. 2013, www.spokesman.com/stories/2013/aug/18/ standardized-tests-popular-with-parents-poll-shows/.

11. To test or not to test; that's a tough question. (2018, March 27). Retrieved June 10, 2020, from https://www.parenttoday. org/to-test-or-not-to-test-thats-a-tough-question/.

12. HOME-SCHOOLING: Outstanding results on national tests. (2009, August 30). Retrieved June 10, 2020, from https://www.washingtontimes.com/news/2009/aug/30/ home-schooling-outstanding-results-national-tests/

13. (n.d.). Retrieved June 10, 2020, from https://nces.ed.gov/ pubs2001/Homeschool/chara.asp

14. (n.d.). Retrieved June 10, 2020, from https://worldpopula- tionreview.com/states/homeschool-laws-by-state/

CHAPTER ELEVEN

1. Skelton, K., Skelton, K., & Organization of Virginia Homeschoolers. (2020, March 26). What Is Accreditation? Should My Homeschool Be Accredited? Retrieved June 11, 2020, from https://www.thehomeschoolmom.com/what-is-accreditation-should-my-homeschool-be-accredited/

CHAPTER TWELVE

1. Mahatma Gandhi Quotes. (n.d.). Retrieved June 11, 2020, from https://www.brainyquote.com/quotes/mahatma_gandhi_150725

CHAPTER THIRTEEN

1. Socialization. (n.d.). Retrieved June 11, 2020, from https://www.sciencedirect.com/topics/social-sciences/socialization.

2. Homeschooling: The Research, Scholarly articles, studies, facts, research. (2020, May 22). Retrieved June 11, 2020, from https://www.nheri.org/research-facts-on-homeschooling/.

3. Cheng, A. (2014). Does Homeschooling or Private Schooling Promote Political Intolerance? Evidence From a Christian University. Journal of School Choice, 8(1), 49-68. doi:10.1080/15582159.2014.875411 from https://www.tandfonline.com/doi/abs/10.1080/15582159.2014.875411#.UzX48dzripp.

About The Author

Laura Kronen believes in living life out loud. Homeschool mother of two, life coach, author, entrepreneur, type 1 diabetic, and founder of lifestyle company Be You Only Better, Laura is always evolving. She is currently on a mission to dispel the stereotypes surrounding homeschooling and to bring home education to the mainstream.

After spending almost two decades working in fashion PR and marketing in New York, Laura ventured out on her own and developed the award-winning children's educational video series Baby Road Trip, as well as the maternity accessory brand, Belly Ups. Ten years ago, she certified to become a life coach and started her company, Be You Only Better, assisting those with self-confidence and self-esteem issues and individuals with entrepreneurial aspirations. She also serves as a mentor for people with diabetes who need help overcoming the challenges of living with the disease.

Besides authoring *Homeschool Happily* and *Too Sweet: The Not-So-Serious Side to Diabetes,* Laura is a lover of wine and tennis (although not at the same time). When not homeschooling her boys or working, she spends her spare time traveling, volunteering, enjoying the sunshine, and buying things in the middle of the night that she doesn't need.

You'll find her eclectic energy all over social media, including on her YouTube channel, *Super Cool Home School,* which features good-vibe educational videos on homeschooling, diabetes, trivia, and sometimes just her stream of consciousness. Reflective of her life, Laura's social networks are an intriguing potpourri, a little bit of everything.

Laura now lives in Atlanta, Georgia, with her husband, their two teenage boys, a rescue cat, two turtles, and an entire ant colony.

Let's Keep the Conversation Going

I hope *Homeschool Happily* has inspired you to join the homeschool community or has given you the encouragement you need to keep going. Please help to spread the word about *Homeschool Happily* by leaving a review on Amazon (amazon. com) or GoodReads (goodreads.com).

Take a visit to my website, **BE YOU ONLY BETTER** (beyouonlybetter.com), to explore my blog. While you are there, check out "My Favorite Things." I have a running list of must-have items that you will soon not be able to live without.

Please also subscribe to my YouTube channel, Super Cool Home School (youtube.com/supercoolhomeschool). I love getting comments on the videos, so let me know what you think or tell me what you would like to see in the future!

If you are on social media, you can find me pretty much everywhere, so please follow me and send me a request. I follow back!

Instagram: @beyouonlybetter   Twitter: @beyouonlybetter
Pinterest: @beyouonlybetter   Facebook: beyouonlybetter
                        YouTube: Super Cool Home School

WISHING YOU SUCCESS AND HAPPINESS ON YOUR HOMESCHOOL ADVENTURE!

Laura

Made in the USA
Columbia, SC
10 July 2020